SpringerBriefs in Philosophy

SpringerBriefs present concise summaries of cutting-edge research and practical applications across a wide spectrum of fields. Featuring compact volumes of 50 to 125 pages, the series covers a range of content from professional to academic. Typical topics might include:

- A timely report of state-of-the art analytical techniques
- A bridge between new research results, as published in journal articles, and a contextual literature review
- A snapshot of a hot or emerging topic
- An in-depth case study or clinical example
- A presentation of core concepts that students must understand in order to make independent contributions

SpringerBriefs in Philosophy cover a broad range of philosophical fields including: Philosophy of Science, Logic, Non-Western Thinking and Western Philosophy. We also consider biographies, full or partial, of key thinkers and pioneers.

SpringerBriefs are characterized by fast, global electronic dissemination, standard publishing contracts, standardized manuscript preparation and formatting guidelines, and expedited production schedules. Both solicited and unsolicited manuscripts are considered for publication in the SpringerBriefs in Philosophy series. Potential authors are warmly invited to complete and submit the Briefs Author Proposal form. All projects will be submitted to editorial review by external advisors.

SpringerBriefs are characterized by expedited production schedules with the aim for publication 8 to 12 weeks after acceptance and fast, global electronic dissemination through our online platform SpringerLink. The standard concise author contracts guarantee that

- an individual ISBN is assigned to each manuscript
- each manuscript is copyrighted in the name of the author
- the author retains the right to post the pre-publication version on his/her website or that of his/her institution.

More information about this series at http://www.springer.com/series/10082

Doris Schroeder · Abol-Hassan Bani-Sadr

Dignity in the 21st Century

Middle East and West

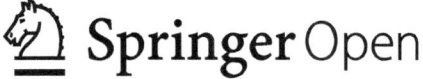

Doris Schroeder
School of Health Sciences,
  College of Health
University of Central Lancashire
Preston
UK

Abol-Hassan Bani-Sadr
Versailles
France

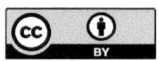

ISSN 2211-4548   ISSN 2211-4556   (electronic)
SpringerBriefs in Philosophy
ISBN 978-3-319-58019-7   ISBN 978-3-319-58020-3   (eBook)
DOI 10.1007/978-3-319-58020-3

Library of Congress Control Number: 2017938529

Printed on acid-free paper

This Springer imprint is published by Springer Nature
The registered company is Springer International Publishing AG
The registered company address is: Gewerbestrasse 11, 6330 Cham, Switzerland

To Inge Mattiat and Uwe Nestler

Doris Schroeder

*To those who stand up for rights,
now and in the future*

Abol-Hassan Bani-Sadr

Foreword

As the editor-in-chief of a bioethics journal, the *Cambridge Quarterly of Healthcare Ethics*, I encounter the concept of dignity regularly and increasingly. I see many treatments of the subject, from efforts to resolve real-life moral dilemmas in health care to highly sophisticated theoretical pieces. More importantly, as a neuroethicist I work on end-of-life issues for those with decreasing mental faculties. The relevance of human dignity does not need explanation in this context. Or does it?

Since Macklin (2003) argued in the *British Medical Journal* that dignity is a useless concept in bioethics, interest in the topic has increased significantly, as have disagreements and disputes over the meaning of 'dignity'.

The idea of conceptualising the topic around the Middle East and West divide is both unique and insightful. It is especially welcome in this time of tensions between the two regions, which infiltrate many areas of our lives.

Doris Schroeder is one of the contemporary bioethicists whose work I most admire. Not only is it consistently well written and clearly argued, but it addresses topics that really matter in the lives of people. Most often she gives a voice to vulnerable populations that are too rarely represented in philosophical discussions. Doris is a philosopher who works *in* the world and is not confined to an ivory tower. She is one of fewer than half a dozen bioethicists writing today whose work I would seek out on any subject.

Until now, I have only been familiar with Bani-Sadr as a political figure in the Middle East. I know of his active part in the anti-Shah student movement in the early 1960s, and his later association with Ayatollah Khomeini that led to his installation as the first President of the Islamic Republic of Iran, ending with his dismissal when he broke with the cleric. Bani-Sadr's standing as a learned scholar of the Koran and his outspoken criticism of violent regimes make him a uniquely qualified commentator, not only on the meaning of dignity in the Islamic tradition, but also on the consequences when power trumps dignity in the current political climate. I was surprised and riveted by his personal memories from the Iran-Iraq war.

Schroeder and Bani-Sadr look at the topic of dignity from very different vantage points: one offers the perspective of Western philosophical analysis, the other the traditional perspective of the Koran. The way in which the two perspectives are finally combined in a call for a concept of dignity that could harmonise the main Western approaches to dignity with the Koranic interpretation is highly instructive: *dignity as respect for and the protection of the self-worth of human beings.*

San Francisco   Professor Thomasine Kushner

Reference

Macklin R (2003) Dignity is a useless concept. BMJ 327:1419−1420

Professor Thomasine Kushner is a philosopher with a special interest in international bioethics. She serves as Director of Neuroethics in the Program *Medicine and Human Values* at California Pacific Medical Center in San Francisco, California. She is founder and editor-in-chief of the *Cambridge Quarterly of Healthcare Ethics* and *Clinical Neuroethics* published by Cambridge University Press. Additionally, she promotes international bioethics by coordinating three annual conferences in Paris: the International Bioethics Retreat, the Cambridge Consortium for Bioethics Education and the Neuroethics Network.

Acknowledgements

Many academic books are written as a deliverable for an external funder. This book, however, was written free of the deadlines and pressure of external funding, and we therefore had all the time in the world to develop our ideas. We are very happy that we finally settled on Springer as our publisher, because the 'SpringerBriefs' format suited our desire to produce a short book that was accessible to a wide audience.

The book goes back to a suggestion by Dr Mahmood Delkhasteh and Dr Miltos Ladikas that Doris might want to comment on an article by Mr Abol-Hassan Bani-Sadr. Mr Bani-Sadr enjoyed Doris' comments, so Mahmood organised a personal meeting in Paris. That was in July 2004! As the book took shape, we communicated through Mahmood and his wife Dr Sarah Amsler, who also translated Mr Bani-Sadr's contributions from Persian and contributed their own ideas. They are both successful academics with heavy workloads and a beautiful young daughter but remained loyal to this project to a degree that astounded and humbled us. Thanks are not enough, and we hope we can somehow reciprocate one day.

This is the fourth book that Prof. Schroeder has published with the guidance of senior Springer editor Fritz Schmuhl—and not the last, as he is quite exceptional. The same applies to our professional copy editor, Paul Wise, whose skills in editing, commenting and finding information are beyond comparison. As both are South Africans, we thank South Africa!

We also had very helpful comments from anonymous referees, whom we thank.

We are very grateful that Doris' friend Prof. Tomi Kushner agreed to write a foreword. Discussions with her and her late husband Dr Mal Kushner were instrumental in forming her views on dignity. She also had several discussions about the book with Prof. Bob Brecher, who was one of those who encouraged her to take the risk of including a fictional dialogue as a conclusion. Hurray to Bob! Thanks also to the College of Health and Wellbeing at the University of Central Lancashire for sponsoring open access for this book.

Others whom Doris would like to thank for very useful discussions about the topic and the book are her husband Armin, Loane Skene, Thomas Pogge, Suzy Killmister, Avner de-Shalit, Roger Chennells, Paul Formosa, Sally Dalton-Brown,

Cathy Lennon, Oliver Sensen, Michael Boylan, Peter Herissone-Kelly, Miltos Ladikas, Julie Cook Lucas, Peter Schaber, Apollonia Jungen (dignity role model), the University of Melbourne Philosophy Seminar, the Queen's College Sugden Lecture audience and the International Bioethics Retreat. Most of the Western part of the book was written in Doris' parents' house—Albert and Mathilde Schroeder. Thanks for the breaks! Last but not least, Doris wants to thank Inge Mattiat and Uwe Nestler, who died—far too early—in 2012, and to whom this book is dedicated.

Mr Bani-Sadr would like to add that in our world, knowledge and science are sometimes used within power relations and sometimes to justify power. People who live life based on rights, who see hope and happiness as intrinsic in life and who succeed in replacing despair with hope, are rare. Dr Sarah Amsler and Dr Mahmood Delkhasteh are among this rare group of people. Mr Bani-Sadr thanks them whole-heartedly.

At a time when violence is taking over life and the dignity of humans and other creations is forgotten, it is a difficult task to invite people to recover their dignity. This book is about the concern that people forget their dignity. It tries to develop a meaning for dignity, so that people can remember what they have lost and through its rediscovery suggest a way of living in independence and freedom. Thank you to our readers for reading it.

Contents

About the Authors

Professor Doris Schroeder whose background is in philosophy, politics and economics, is Director of the Centre for Professional Ethics at the University of Central Lancashire (UCLan) in the UK, Professor of Moral Philosophy in the School of Law at UCLan Cyprus, and Adjunct Professor at Charles Sturt University in Canberra, Australia. Professor Schroeder has published and led large international research projects on benefit sharing, responsible research and innovation, and global research ethics. Her conceptual work in ethics focuses mostly on the human right of access to health care, dignity and vulnerability.

Abol-Hassan Bani-Sadr was Iran's first president from 1980 to 1981, when he was overthrown in a coup. In addition to theorising the 1979 Iranian Revolution, he has published a wide range of books and articles in the fields of philosophy, theology, sociology and economics. His work centres around critiquing traditional and fundamentalist forms of Islam and, through in-depth study of the Koran, constructing revolutionary new interpretations of Islam as discourses of liberty which prioritise freedom, dignity and human rights. Key works, in Persian, include *The Cult of Personality; The Koran: The Book of Discourse of Independence and Freedom; Free Intellect; Social Justice, Totalitarianism;* and *The Foundation of Democracy.*

Chapter 1
The Quest for Dignity

There is no cultural system, Western or non-Western, however new or however old, that fully lives up to the idea of human dignity.

Wood (2008: 64)

Abstract Dignity is a highly controversial concept. Few other terms have been used in so many settings with so many contradictory meanings. Political events in the Middle East have given dignity new meanings. Some analysts have gone as far as calling the revolutions and civil wars that have dominated this region in the early 21st century the 'dignity revolutions'. With this book we want to show that the concept of dignity can be meaningfully employed in politics, philosophy and everyday life, if one is clear about its different meanings, and about which of those meanings to use in what context.

Keywords Dignity · Dignity revolutions

It is difficult to write about dignity. Few other terms have been used in so many settings with so many contradictory meanings.

On the one hand, it is proclaimed that dignity[1] can never be lost. 'Dignity is inviolable' is the first sentence of the German constitution, to give an example. On the other hand, movements around the world declare that they are on a mission to *acquire* dignity for their constituencies. From Syrian refugee girls (UNICEF 2015) to government commissions investigating the neglect and abuse of elderly residents in care homes (Age UK n.d.), politicians and activists have used the term to support their quests.

Swiss philosopher and novelist Peter Bieri (also known as Pascal Mercier) captured some of the mysteries of the term 'dignity' in his novel *Night Train to Lisbon*. The novel sees middle-aged teacher Gregorius abandon his post and travel to Lisbon. There he meets a former resistance fighter, João Eça, who lives in a

---

[1]The terms 'dignity' and 'human dignity' are used interchangeably in this book.

© The Author(s) 2017
D. Schroeder and A. Bani-Sadr, *Dignity in the 21st Century*,
SpringerBriefs in Philosophy, DOI 10.1007/978-3-319-58020-3_1

nursing home. One day, João Eça is reluctant to receive Gregorius for their regular chess meetings.

> When João Eça stood in the door of his room … on Sunday, Gregorius saw in his face that something had happened. Eça hesitated before asking him in. It was a cold March day, yet the window was wide open.…
>
> Eça moved the pawns. 'I went in bed last night,' he said in a rough voice. 'And I didn't notice it.' He kept his eyes lowered to the board.…
>
> Gregorius made tea and poured him half a cup. Eça saw the look that fell on his shaking hands.
>
> '*A dignidade*,' he said.
>
> 'Dignity,' said Gregorius. 'I have no idea what that really is. But I don't think it's something that gets lost just because the body fails.'
>
> Eça botched the opening.
>
> 'When they led me to torture, I went in my pants and they laughed at it. It was a horrible *humiliation*; but I didn't feel I was losing my *dignity*. But what is it *then*?'
>
> Did he believe he would lose his dignity if he had talked, asked Gregorius.
>
> 'I didn't say a word, not a single word. I locked away all the possible words in me. Yes, that's it: I *locked* them away and bolted the door irrevocably. So it was *impossible* for me to talk. … I stopped acknowledging the torturers as actors. They didn't know it, but I degraded them. …'
>
> And if they had loosened his tongue with a drug?
>
> He had often asked himself that, said Eça, and he had dreamed of it. He had come to the conclusion that they could have *destroyed* him with that, but they could never take away his *dignity* in this way. To lose your dignity, you had to *forfeit* yourself.
>
> 'And then you get worked up about a dirtied bed?' said Gregorius and shut the window. 'It's cold and it doesn't smell, not at all.' (Mercier 2009: 364−365)

João Eça believes that he kept his dignity during torture and that the torturers could never have taken it from him. Yet he also believes that he lost his dignity when he 'went in bed'. His chess partner Gregorius admits that he has no idea what dignity really means, but insists that it does not get lost when the body begins to fail. The interpretations of dignity that this short excerpt point to are already quite diverse. One is connected to willpower and effort (resisting torturers), the other is independent of either and refers only to the frailty of the ageing human body.

This book aims to illuminate the concept of dignity in the 21st century.[2] What does it mean in the West? What does it mean in the Middle East? And could there be a common understanding? Or is there a common essence? Our attempt to answer these questions from a Western perspective will be done from a broad base, which includes fiction, politics and everyday life (e.g. sports), as well as the philosophical literature. There are three reasons for doing so:

---

[2]For more information on our exact Western and Middle Eastern perspectives, please see Box 1.1 at the end of this chapter.

1. Using examples from a wide range of contexts highlights vividly why the concept of dignity is so contentious in the 21st century.
2. Dignity has become a popular topic in philosophy, and many excellent books that engage critically with a broad range of interpretations have been published recently.[3] To add one that simply covers the same ground would probably not be very useful.
3. The concept is so important in everyday life, as the many examples will show, that the discussion is intended not just for a specialised audience, but general readers too.

One could ask: why draw a distinction between dignity in the Middle East and dignity in the West? Why not assume that we can agree on *one* universal concept, as envisaged by the drafters of the Universal Declaration of Human Rights in 1948 (UN 1948)? To make this assumption would be to ignore the continuing heated debates about the essence of dignity. It would also not make the concept any clearer. If one had to pack everything that people could mean by 'dignity' into one concept, that concept might become meaningless. Any serious effort to describe dignity therefore has to disentangle different meanings first, and only then ask whether some of these meanings could be reconciled.

While it may be desirable to strive for a universal understanding of dignity, in that it could facilitate intercultural dialogue, one of our reasons for writing this book is that dignity is too multifaceted a concept to be captured in one essence. Instead we strive to bring out the distinctions *within* Western concepts and then provide one Middle Eastern interpretation. This is necessary because dignity is one of the most controversial concepts of the 20th and 21st centuries. It has been described as powerful (Beyleveld and Brownsword 2001), yet useless and vague (Macklin 2003); arbitrary (Van Steendam et al. 2006), yet addictive (Wetz 2004); elusive (Ullrich 2003), yet widely used (Van Steendam et al. 2006); groundless (Rachels 1990), yet revolutionary (Wood 2008); of supreme importance, yet without reference point.[4] And this is just a summary of Western academic debates (Fig. 1.1).

Within this confusion, one looks to the Middle East and realises that political events have given dignity new meanings. Some analysts have gone as far as calling the revolutions and civil wars that have dominated this region in the early 21st century the 'dignity revolutions' (Hassan 2011).

While rising food prices, poverty, unemployment and corruption have contributed to these uprisings, commentators in the region and around the world have spoken of a dignity uprising: 'ordinary Tunisians, Libyans, and Egyptians themselves describe the heart of this moment as a revolution for dignity' (Marquand 2011). 'But the uprisings were not only about jobs and bread; as Sudanese intellectual Abdelwahab El-Affendi wrote, … the revolutions were needed so that the

---

[3]We would recommend, for instance, Michael Rosen's *Dignity: Its History and Meaning* for English-speaking readers and Peter Schaber's *Menschenwürde* for German-speakers.

[4]Statman (2000: 536) refers to 'legal discourse, in which, on the one hand, dignity is assigned supreme importance, but, on the other, it has no clear reference'.

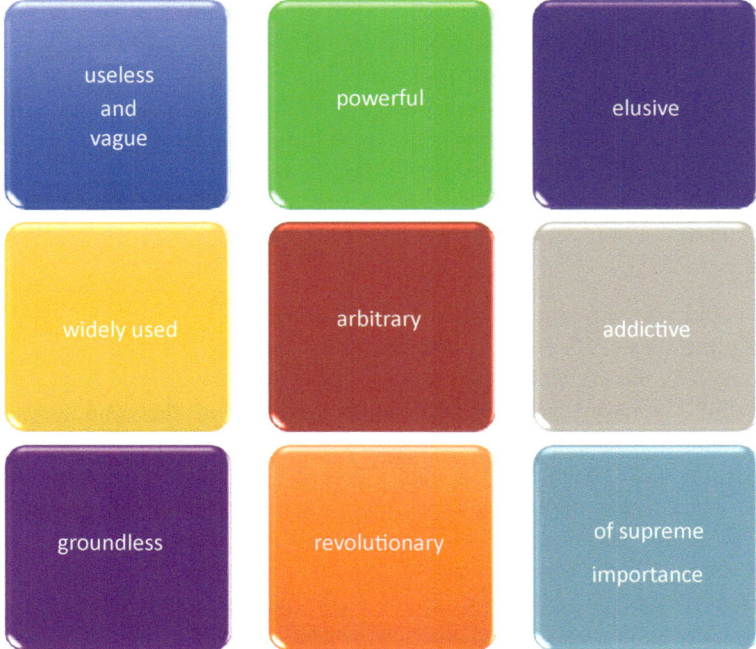

Fig. 1.1 Judgements on the concept of dignity

people would deserve bread' (Lynch 2011). The theme of restoring the dignity of the people pervaded the Arab uprisings. 'Some will claim that the true, structural causes for these Arab revolts reside in the rising food prices or other objective economic factors. … But that is not what the street interviewees and commentators tell us: they speak of Anger, of Pride, of Humiliation and Dignity' (De Cauter 2011). Or, as Fukuyama (2012) put it in an editorial entitled *The Drive for Dignity*:

> The basic issue was one of *dignity*, or the lack thereof, the feeling of worth or self-esteem that all of us seek. But dignity is not felt unless it is *recognized* by other people; it is an inherently social and, indeed, political phenomenon. The Tunisian police were treating Bouazizi[5] as a nonperson, someone not worthy of the basic courtesy of a reply or explanation when the government took away his modest means of livelihood.

The concept of dignity (Arabic *karama*) has often been used to comment on events in the Middle East. While dignity hardly ever featured in previous uprisings around the world, it is a 'core theme… of the Arab uprisings, which united Arabs

---

[5]On 17 December 2010, Tunisian street vendor Mohamed Bouazizi set fire to himself in protest at the harassment and humiliation inflicted on him by a municipal officer and her colleagues. He died from severe burns 18 days later, without waking up from his coma. He was posthumously awarded the Sakharov Prize for Freedom of Thought by the European Parliament (with four others), and the Times named him their person of the year for 2011. His death sparked protests in Tunisia that 'legend … has it … kicked off … the Arab Spring' (Fukuyama 2012).

from Morocco to Oman' (Hashemi 2013b). Commentators speak of a collective 'assertion of self-dignity in the Arab world' (Ilan Pappé in Barat 2011) after 'decades of humiliation, despotism, and despair' (Hashemi 2013a: 229) (see also Khouri 2011). It is therefore the right time to look at the concept of dignity in the Middle East.

Illuminating the concept from both a Western *and* a Middle Eastern perspective will, we hope, also increase its clarity. While Western academic attacks on the concept might have a point (more in Sect. 2.5.1 on the 'vagueness' of dignity), the concept's power in everyday life is considerable, as are the potential tediousness and philosophical sophistry of any alternatives. The following brief excerpt from an Australian novel could help illuminate this point:

> Girlie had a new English teacher, an untidy, pimply young woman named Miss Boatwright, whom she couldn't stand. She became as impatient as her mother, shooting up her hand to point out the teacher's errors, creating disturbances, generally being delinquent. At recess, she made fun of the half-moons of sweat that stained the armpits of Miss Boatwright's frocks…. Miss Boatwright's efforts at salvaging her dignity only made Girlie more scornful. (Jennings 1996: 112)

The reader is flooded with images by just four sentences: images of pupils, teachers, classrooms and, at another level, images of desolation and loneliness. They will see that the schoolgirl lacks kindness, empathy, generosity and compassion. They may feel sorry for the teacher or think she should have chosen a different profession. But any attempt to find another, equally powerful formulation to replace the phrase 'salvaging her dignity' is likely to be fruitless. The power of the paragraph lies in this term and all its connotations. 'Miss Boatwright's efforts at salvaging her right to respect for persons and their autonomy only made Girlie more scornful' just sounds dull and wearisome.

With this book we want to show that the concept of dignity can be meaningfully employed in politics, philosophy and everyday life, if one is clear about its different meanings, and about which of those meanings to use in what context.

Box 1.1 West? Middle East?

We are two authors from different cultures. One born and raised in Cologne, Germany and one born and raised in Hamadan, Iran. This gives us certain perspectives, but that is not the reason why the sub-title of the book is "Middle East and West".

We agreed this subtitle for three reasons.

First, the "Western part" of the book uses so many different, mostly Western sources, from Aristotle to Kant, from Iris Murdoch to Paul Auster, from European newspapers to Internet sports pages, from the German constitution to American court cases, from psychology to Catholicism that a more precise specification was not possible.

Second, the "Middle Eastern part" of the book relies almost exclusively on the Koran, a book which conquered the world from its Middle Eastern origins.

Third, the interpretation of dignity in light of the Koran presented in this book, is unusual, and could not be linked to either Shia or Sunni Islam interpretations.[6] Bani-Sadr argues—using the Koran—that Western and Middle Eastern challenges today (e.g. the rise of ultra-right and populist movements in the West and the strong authoritarian tendencies within Islamic societies) have the same root: a distinction between "good power" and "bad power" His interpretation of dignity, on the other hand, assumes that power invariably results in domination and one cannot have "good domination" and "bad domination", since domination is always a negation of human dignity and human rights.

In a conversation Bani-Sadr said: "It was around 40 years ago when I began my research for finding the roots of dignity in Western philosophy. That led me to Giovanni Pico della Mirandola, and his Oration of the Dignity of Man. He starts his treatise by stating: 'Most esteemed Fathers, I have read in the ancient writings of the Arabians that Abdala the Saracen on being asked what, on this stage, so to say, of the world, seemed to him most evocative of wonder, replied that there was nothing to be seen more marvelous than man.'

The Arab man whom he is referring to is Ali, the fourth Caliph after the prophet Mohammed and the first Shia Imam in the 7th century. That led me to go back to the Koran and start my research about dignity and where, how and why the word is being used and what it actually means. There I found that all living beings have dignity and rights because they are created by God. To bring out the dignity in all beings requires that the discourse of power and domination is replaced by a discourse of freedom and independence.

My suggestion to thinkers within varies belief systems and discourses is to try to discover the discourse of freedom and independence, within their own belief system."

Hence, the subtitle of this book is "Middle East and West" because the sources used cannot be traced to any more precise discourses (e.g. a solely Kantian approach or reliance on a Shia interpretation of the Koran).

References

Age UK (n.d.) Improving dignity in care. http://www.ageuk.org.uk/home-and-care/improving-dignity-in-care-consultation/

---

[6]Sunni and Shia Islam are the two major denominations of Islam. The vast majority of Muslims today are Sunni, with Shia being the majority only in the area of ancient Persia, e.g. Iran and Iraq. Members of the two denominations "have co-existed for centuries and share many fundamental beliefs and practices. But they differ in doctrine, ritual, law, theology and religious organisation." For more information see http://www.bbc.com/news/world-middle-east-16047709.

Barat F (2011) Reframing the Israel-Palestine conflict. New Internationalist Magazine, 1 April 2011. https://newint.org/features/web-exclusive/2011/04/01/palestine-israel-interview-pappe/

Beyleveld D, Brownsword R (2001) Human dignity in bioethics and biolaw. Oxford University Press, Oxford

De Cauter L (2011) The days of anger: Humiliation, fear and dignity in the Middle East. Foreign Policy in Focus, 8 April. http://fpif.org/the_days_of_anger_humiliation_fear_and_dignity_in_the_middle_east/

Fukuyama F (2012) The drive for dignity. Foreign Policy, 12 January. http://foreignpolicy.com/2012/01/12/the-drive-for-dignity/

Hashemi N (2013a) Syria, savagery, and self-determination: What those against military inter-vention are missing. In: Hashemi N, Postel D (eds) The Syria dilemma. Massachusetts In-stitute of Technology, Cambridge MA, p 221–236

Hashemi N (2013b) The Arab Spring two years on: Reflections on dignity, democracy, and devotion. Ethics and International Affairs 27(2):207–221

Hassan K (2011) Regional perspectives on the 'dignity revolutions': How Middle Eastern ac-tivists perceive popular protest. Knowledge Programme Civil Society In West Asia, Policy Paper 3. University of Amsterdam; Hivos, The Hague. https://www.hivos.org/sites/default/files/publications/465733.pdf

Hospital JT (1990) History is false but this is true. The New York Times, 25 March. http://www.nytimes.com/1990/03/25/books/history-is-false-but-this-is-true.html

Jennings K (1996) Snake. Minerva, Melbourne

Khouri RG (2011) The long revolt. The Wilson Quarterly 35(2):43–46

Lynch M (2011) The big think behind the Arab Spring: Do the Middle East's revolutions have a unifying ideology? Foreign Policy, 28 November http://foreignpolicy.com/2011/11/28/the-big-think-behind-the-arab-spring/

Macklin R (2003) Dignity is a useless concept. BMJ 327:1419–1420

Marquand R (2011) At the heart of the Arab revolts: A search for dignity. Christian Science Monitor, 3 March. http://www.csmonitor.com/World/Middle-East/2011/0303/At-the-heart-of-the-Arab-revolts-a-search-for-dignity

Mercier P (2009) Night train to Lisbon. Atlantic Books, London

Rachels J (1990) Created from animals: The moral implications of Darwinism. Oxford University Press, New York

Statman D (2000) Humiliation, dignity and self-respect. Philosophical Psychology 13(4):523–540

Ullrich D (2003) Concurring visions: Human dignity in the Canadian Charter of Rights and Freedoms and the Basic Law of the Federal Republic of Germany. Global Jurist Frontiers 3 (1):17

UN (1948) Universal Declaration of Human Rights. United Nations. http://www.un.org/en/universal-declaration-human-rights/

UNICEF (2015) 'Enough pain': A Syrian refugee girl pleads for dignity. http://www.un.org/youthenvoy/2015/10/enough-pain-syrian-refugee-girl-pleads-dignity-unicef/

Van Steendam G, Dinnyés A, Mallet J, Meloni R, Romeo Casabona C, Guerra Gonzáles J, Kuře J, Szathmáry E, Vorstenbosch J, Molnár P, Edbrooke D, Sándor J, Oberfrank F, Cole-Turner R, Hargittai I, Littig B, Ladikas M, Mordini E, Roosendaal HE, Salvi M, Gulyás B, Malpede D (2006) Summary: The Budapest Meeting 2005 intensified networking on ethics of science: The case of reproductive cloning, germline gene therapy, and human dignity. Sci Eng Ethics 12 (4):731–793

Wetz FJ (2004) Menschenwürde als Opium fürs Volk: Der Wertstatus von Embryonen. In: Kettner M (ed) Biomedizin und Menschenwürde. Edition Suhrkamp, Frankfurt, p 221–248

Wood A (2008) Human dignity, right and the realm of ends. Acta Juridica i:47–65

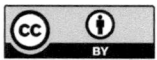

Chapter 2
Dignity in the West

People must not be humiliated, that is the main thing.
Anton Chekhov, 1887 (Hospital 1990)

Abstract What is dignity from a Western perspective? This chapter provides a short history of dignity in the West, focusing on Immanuel Kant's concept of dignity, dignity in legal instruments and dignity in bioethics supplemented by fiction, politics and everyday life (e.g. sports). A taxonomy of dignity is developed and illustrated in a diagram.

Keywords Dignity · Kant · Bioethics · Virtue · Self-worth

2.1 Introduction

What is dignity from a Western perspective? The answer to this question covers such a vast area that a focus is needed, and this will be provided through two riddles (Fig. 2.1). One is a riddle of law or political science, the other a riddle of moral theory.

Riddle 1: The German constitution states in article 1(1) that 'human dignity is inviolable' *and* that 'its protection is the duty of all state powers' (Germany 1949: art. 1 I, DS translation). Why would something that is *inviolable* (meaning secure from attack, assault or trespass) need protection?[1]

---

[1] Of course the verb in 'Die Würde des Mensch *ist* unantastbar' should normally be translated with 'is' (human dignity *is* inviolable), if the aim of translation is to translate, and not to interpret. However, sometimes the verb is given as 'shall' in English translation: 'Human dignity shall be inviolable.' This is presumably done to resolve the riddle. Since this book is not a text in jurisprudence and the riddle is only used for illustrative purposes, it is easy to justify using a literal translation here. Note that 'is' is also used in the English text written by the German Federal Government Commissioner for Human Rights Policy at http://www.young-germany.de/topic/live/life-style/human-dignity-is-inviolable.

© The Author(s) 2017
D. Schroeder and A. Bani-Sadr, *Dignity in the 21st Century*,
SpringerBriefs in Philosophy, DOI 10.1007/978-3-319-58020-3_2

Fig. 2.1 Dignity riddles

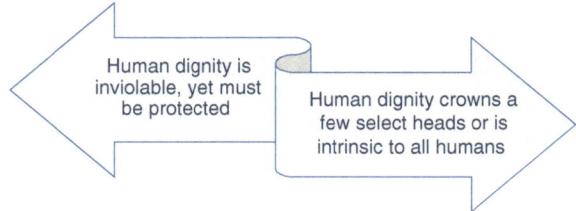

Table 2.1 Dignity: synonyms and related concepts (Thesaurus. Microsoft Word 1997–2003)

Decorum	Formality	Nobility	Self-respect
Restraint	Reserve	Graciousness	Self-esteem
Good manners	Stiffness	Decency	Self-worth
Modesty	Primness	Nobleness	Pride
Etiquette	Correctness	Goodness	Confidence

Riddle 2:   Who is right? According to Germany's most famous poet, Johann Wolfgang von Goethe (1749–1832), 'a laurel is much easier bound than a dignified head for it found'.[2] In other words, dignity crowns only a few select heads. But according to Germany's most famous philosopher, Immanuel Kant (1724–1804), dignity is intrinsic and cannot be denied even to a vicious man (more on this in Sect. 2.4.4.1) (Kant 1990: 110 [463], DS translation). In other words, dignity is not selective: in Kant's interpretation, it belongs to all human beings

The riddles will be used to distinguish between different meanings of dignity in the West, looking not only at academic debates, but also at the term's historical meaning, its use in legal instruments and its occurrence in fiction, as well as in political and everyday life (Fig. 2.1).

Most Western and northern European expressions for dignity go back to the Latin *dignitas* (*dignité, dignità, dignidade, dignidad, dignity*)[3] or the Old German *wirdî* (*Würde, waardigheid, värdighet*).[4]

> The Latin term *dignitas* itself is directly related to the Latin noun *decus*, which means ornament, distinction, honour or glory. The equivalent verb *decet* can be linked to the Greek term *dokein*, which means to show or to seem (Lebech 2004).

If one looks for synonyms of dignity, in order better to understand the term, the following suggest themselves: decorum, formality, nobility and self-respect—and each of these nouns has others associated with it, as the following table shows (Table 2.1).

---

[2]Translation by one of the authors (DS) from the German: 'Ein Kranz ist gar viel leichter binden, als ihm ein würdig Haupt zu finden' (Goethe n.d.).

[3]French, Italian, Portuguese, Spanish, English.

[4]German, Dutch, Swedish.

Looking at the terms in the above table, one could already arrive at a solution to one of the two riddles: Goethe is right, dignity is something that does not crown every head. To be modest, restrained, correct, noble, confident and so on is *not* an *intrinsic* property of all human beings. These are characteristics to which humans may *aspire*. One would also have to conclude that the protection of dignity by state powers, as noted in the German constitution, does not make sense if good manners, graciousness and correctness are among possible synonyms.

Let us see whether the term's use in everyday life and fiction can provide more clues for the riddles.

2.2 Dignity's Omnipresence

The term 'dignity' can be found in legal documents, politics, fiction and various aspects of everyday life. Once one starts looking, it seems omnipresent.

In sports, a journalist writing for a New Zealand outlet summed up the 2015 Rugby World Cup under the headling 'Northern hemisphere rugby has lost its dignity'. He wrote: 'Northern hemisphere rugby has exited the 2015 World Cup with the same haste and dignity as referee Craig Joubert's sprint for the toilet' (Reason 2015).

Just under ten years earlier, a football event so enraged journalists that commentators used the term 'dignity' in entirely contradictory interpretations. In the final of the 2006 FIFA World Cup, the captain of the French team, Zinedine Zidane, attacked a member of the Italian team, Marco Materazzi, ramming his head into Materazzi's chest. Zidane later alleged that Materazzi had made defamatory comments about his mother and sister. The next day, the German regional newspaper *Kölner Stadt-Anzeiger* led its sport section with a headline declaring that a great player had lost his dignity (Löer 2006). At the same time, the Parisian newspaper *Le Nouvel Observateur* noted that Zidane's head-butt was an existential act, as 'dignity is more important than sport. You do not swallow an insult' (Dart 2006). The German journalist may have thought of dignity in the context of restraining one's temper, showing good manners, being modest, reserved and correct: all possible synonyms of dignity from Table 2.1. The French journalist might have thought of dignity as standing up for one's family's pride, defending their self-worth and so on: other synonyms from Table 2.1. But even without surmising what the journalists thought, it is clear that their interpretation of dignity was characteristics-based. Their judgements would not make any sense if dignity were inviolable and all human beings possessed it. With regard to the first puzzle, Goethe would be right. Dignity crowns only a few select heads and it is an effort to be thus worthy.

In 2015 and 2016, the term was used often in the context of the refugee movements from the Middle East and across the Mediterranean sea. For instance, a member of the European Parliament (MEP) wrote the following in a British newspaper:

This international crisis needs an international response. The European Union and its member states should avoid finger pointing. It is high time to manage the refugee crisis. Only a common European solution will be the answer to the diverse internal and external cross-border challenges we face. This is first of all a matter of humanity and of human dignity. And for Europe it is also a matter of historical fairness (McAllister 2015).

Whose dignity is at stake and what dignity means in the context of the refugee crisis is not clear from this quotation, but many readers may have sympathised with the MEP's call for action.

There is more that one can quote from the fields of politics and human rights activism. Nelson Mandela said:

It should never be that the anger of the poor should be the finger of accusation pointed at all of us because we failed to respond to the cries of the people for food, for shelter, for the dignity of the individual (Crwys-Williams 1997: 62).

Former Norwegian Minister of International Development Hilde F. Johnson expressed the same belief:

We have but one world and one measure of the value of human dignity. Extreme poverty is a violation of human dignity (Johnson 2005: 21).

In his request, Mandela asks the affluent and comfortable to respond to the cries of the poor and help provide food and shelter. It is unclear how dignity fits into this appeal. By referring to food, shelter and dignity together, he almost seems to suggest that the affluent could give dignity to the poor, just as they can give food and shelter. This fits neither of the dignity riddles. Dignity is then not an inviolable property of all human beings, which cannot be lost. If it were, it could not be given to the poor. Nor is it a property that human beings obtain through merit (Goethe), if it can be given by some to others, and if the only reason the givers are in the position to do so is that they are affluent. One could possibly venture that Mandela uses the term emotively here, in exhorting the affluent to assist the poor, but this is done at the expense of clarity.

Likewise Johnson: had she said that extreme poverty was a violation of human rights, it would arguably have been a clearer claim than the claim that dignity is being violated. For instance, article 25(1) of the Universal Declaration of Human Rights proclaims that:

Everyone has the right to a standard of living adequate for the health and well-being of himself and of his family, including food, clothing, housing and medical care and necessary social services, and the right to security in the event of unemployment, sickness, disability, widowhood, old age or other lack of livelihood in circumstances beyond his control (UN 1948).

Those living in extreme poverty do not have a standard of living adequate for their health and well-being, because they lack food, clothing, housing, and medical and social care. But if extreme poverty were a violation of human dignity, as Johnson notes, would this mean that human dignity and human rights were identical? If so, why use a term (dignity) that is less clear (Schroeder 2012)?

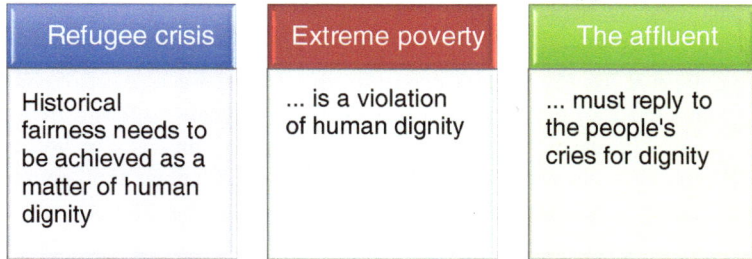

Fig. 2.2 Dignity in recent politics

While the Mandela and Johnson quotes do not immediately help with the riddles, one can see a glimpse of something that might be important. As Avishai Margalit has noted, it is easier to understand negative concepts than positive ones. For instance, 'it is easier to identify humiliating than respectful behaviour, just as it is easier to identify illness than health' (Margalit 1998: 5). One could venture that Mandela and Johnson are pointing towards the circumstances of extreme poverty, where the lack of food and shelter make it extraordinarily difficult to maintain the value of human dignity, for instance by being able to resist coercive offers (and to maintain honesty and integrity) (Fig. 2.2).

Moving from politics to literature, Paul Ricoeur has remarked that 'literature proves to consist in a vast laboratory for thought experiments' (Ricoeur 1995: 148). A range of quotations from literature involving dignity will be presented to show the concept's omnipresence, and also to move forward with the two riddles.

> Her gloves, as Razumihin noticed, were not merely shabby but had holes in them, and yet this evident poverty gave the two ladies an air of special dignity, which is always found in people who know how to wear poor clothes. Razumihin looked reverently at Dounia and felt proud of escorting her. 'The queen who mended her stockings in prison,' he thought, 'must have looked then every inch a queen and even more a queen than at sumptuous banquets and levées.' (Dostoevsky 1917)

Fyodor Dostoevsky's short description of two ladies who have fallen into poverty is highly evocative thanks to his use of the term 'dignity'. It conjures up an image of quiet pride and resilience in the face of hardship, as well as a sense of preserved self-esteem. While Dostoevsky does not speak of extreme poverty, as Mandela and Johnson do, it is noticeable that he ascribes dignity to a way of coping with poverty. Thus, going back to the two riddles, Goethe rather than Kant would be right in claiming that dignity requires effort and striving.

> They had always been very close to each other, united by indistinguishable close bonds of love and intelligence … They had never seriously quarrelled, never been parted, never doubted each other's complete honesty … Their love had grown, nourished daily by the liveliness of their shared thoughts. They had grown together in mind and body and soul as it is sometimes blessedly given to two people to do …. Certain subjects the instincts of their affections made taboo. They never spoke later of the lost child. … Though they were playfully and demonstrably loving together they kept a rein upon certain runs or courses of

sentiment. Their language was chaste and there was a reticent dignity in their love. (Murdoch 1980: 21f)

The picture that Iris Murdoch draws with this paragraph is of a couple who lead a quiet, contented life, united rather than destroyed by the suffering of losing a child, a couple who carry their pain with dignity. Again, this way of life requires resilience and effort and cannot be ascribed to all human beings, thus giving more weight to Goethe's insights rather than Kant's.

'A man's love is a fire of olive-wood. It leaps higher every moment; it roars, it blazes, it shoots out red flames; it threatens to wrap you round and devour you – you who stand by like an icicle in the glow of its fierce warmth. You are self-reproached at your own chilliness and want of reciprocity. The next day, when you go to warm your hands a little, you find a few ashes!' ... 'You speak so because you do not know men,' said Em, instantly assuming the dignity of superior knowledge so universally affected by affianced and married women in discussing man's nature with their uncontracted sisters. (Schreiner 1989: 167)

Olive Schreiner uses the term 'dignity' to describe the potentially pretentious feelings of superiority that married women have over their unmarried 'sisters'. She thereby uses the term to refer to a particular status that one group has achieved simply by virtue of its position. Such a position might be reached with effort, but positions can also be achieved without any effort. For instance, a woman whose parents are very rich might find it easier to join the club of 'contracted sisters', as Schreiner calls them.

Early in our friendship, Trause told me a story about a French writer he had known in Paris in the early fifties. I can't remember his name, but John said ... [he] was considered to be one of the shining lights of the young generation. He also wrote some poetry, and not long before John returned to America ... this writer acquaintance published a book-length narrative poem that revolved around the drowning death of a young child. Two months after the book was released, the writer and his family went on a vacation to the Normandy coast, and on the last day of their trip his five-year-old daughter waded out into the choppy waters of the English Channel and drowned. The writer was a rational man, John said, a person known for his lucidity and sharpness of mind, but he blamed the poem for his daughter's death. Lost in the throes of grief, he persuaded himself that the words he'd written about an imaginary drowning had caused a real drowning .... As a consequence, this immensely gifted writer, this man who had been born to write books, vowed never to write again ... When John told me the story, the daughter had been dead for twenty-one years, and the writer still hadn't broken his vow. In French literary circles, that silence had turned him into a legendary figure. He was held in the highest regard for the dignity of his suffering, pitied by all who knew him, looked upon with awe. (Auster 2004: 187f)

According to Paul Auster, those who knew the French author who had lost his daughter looked upon him with awe. This awe stemmed from admiration of his strength to deal with suffering in a dignified manner: to stick steadfastly to his belief that he should no longer write, while carrying his burden with poise. Clearly Goethe rather than Kant speaks from this quote. Dignity crowns only a few select heads.

Christoph Kömüves' hair had greyed prematurely since he was promoted to the central office. He had gained a little weight and his bodily condition was not pleasant to him. ... Even though he could not settle on one of those modern diets, as he felt they were girlish

..., he caught himself from time to time thinking about his body. Yes, he appeared older than he was, almost a gentleman of mature age ... with grey hair and the beginnings of a belly. Sometimes he joked about it with good friends, who replied: 'A belly means esteem.' This comforted him, as he always endeavoured to exude dignity ... to distract from his youth. (Márai 2005: 19f, DS translation)

Sándor Márai's use of dignity seems to be concerned mostly with appearances. For his character, Christoph Kömüves, dignity seems to equate with maturity in age and a stature that creates esteem. If a belly can be linked to dignity, it is neither a universal feature nor one that, in most cases, requires special effort and striving.

He had not slept a wink, and he felt better for it; in fact he was quite sure ... that he would never want to sleep again. His lips curled in an involuntary sneer as he looked around the train carriage and saw how many of the passengers were already – so early in the day! – either dozing, or napping, or nodding off, or snoozing, or snatching forty winks, their mouths hanging stupidly open, their heads lolling, their eyelids drooping heavily. Did these people have no sense of dignity, no self-respect? (Coe 1997: 312).

Coe introduces the reader to a character who is indignant at a particular habit he finds undignified, namely sleeping in public. Instead of keeping up appearances, the travellers nod off and show such undignified sides of themselves as open mouths and lolling heads—comportment they could have refrained from with a little effort. The narrator therefore sides with Goethe in seeing dignity as a selective property (Fig. 2.3).

What the above figures from literary fiction have in common is this: either they have a certain position or appearance that leads to the external perception of dignity or lack thereof (the married woman, the greying office worker, the snoozing passenger), or they make an effort, sometimes a heroic effort, to preserve their dignity (the Russian ladies, the loving couple, the grieving poet). In all instances, dignity is

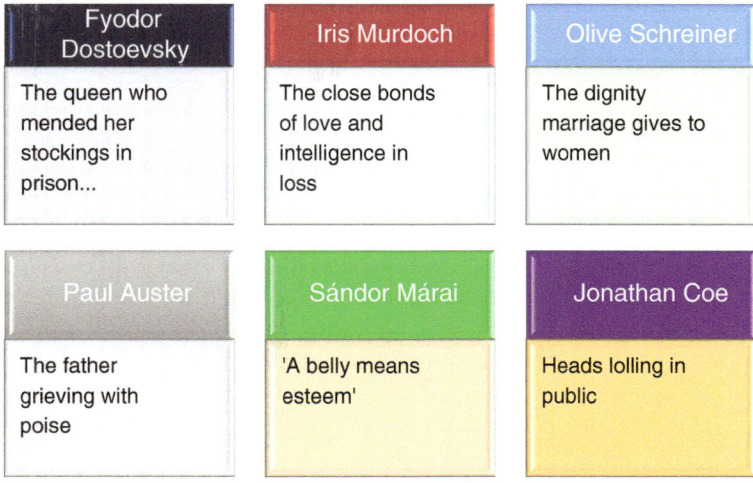

Fig. 2.3 Dignity in literature

something one can aspire to that could lead to a laurel, as in Goethe's poem, if achieved. It is not something intrinsic in humankind, as the German constitution, via the earlier riddle, assumes.

If somebody from a culture that does not have a word for dignity is learning English, would the above help her understand the concept? In some respects yes. She would probably come to the conclusion that, in most cases, authors use the term as a descriptive property. Among other things, characters can be humble, modest, pleasant, charming, plain, lazy, mean, vicious, aggressive, serene, and—dignified. They can demonstrate intelligence, beauty, arrogance, pride, languor, humility and—dignity. In almost all of the quotes above, one learns something about particular human beings that sets them apart from others; some show dignity, others do not. If dignity were an inherent property of all human beings, it would have no useful meaning in fiction. No author would use it to describe their characters, as it would not set them apart from others. The phrase 'a dignified old lady' would be identical in meaning to the phrase 'an old lady'. This is clearly not the case. Bertolt Brecht's short story 'Die unwuerdige Greisin',[5] about an allegedly undignified old lady, would not make sense.

Hence, in fiction and poetry, dignity is a useful descriptor precisely because some people display it and others do not. Judged from its use in the above quotes alone, dignity would seem to be a property that is not inherent in all human beings; it can be seen and recognised, but not all humans possess it. Therefore dignity does not seem to be inviolable and intrinsic. Its presentation in the quotations above comes down firmly on the side of the first riddle. Of course, the selection of excerpts might have been highly selective, designed to give that impression—and besides, these quotations are too few to represent the breadth required for the blanket conclusions to be drawn. But one can say that in fiction, at least sometimes, dignity is used as a descriptive property which sets people apart, as opposed to a property that applies universally to humankind.

The following two excerpts show the use of dignity in fiction in a much broader way than in the earlier examples.

> I found a run-down café. ... I sat there for an hour. I thought that somewhere in the universe must lie the other world ... a sun-golden world, a dignified world. Where every human found the one meant for them, where every love was true love and where one lived eternally. And, of course, I immediately thought of those who could not live even there; who were not suited for such generous, sumptuous grace. The damned, who would take their own lives even there. (Grossman 2003: 250, DS translation).

Grossman invokes the image of an ideal world, where everybody finds true love and lives eternally. He decides to call this a dignified world. He thus equates dignity with perfection, ideals, dreams, a sun-golden world. This excerpt from fiction would probably please opponents of the concept of dignity. To equate everything

---

[5]Strangely, the English translation of the story gives 'unseemly' rather than 'undignified' for 'unwürdig' (Brecht 2003: 144). The German equivalent of 'unseemly' is 'unziemlich' or 'unpassend', which is only partly related to dignity.

perfect and ideal with dignity makes it either very vague (what does 'perfect' or 'ideal' mean exactly?) or superfluous (if one knows what 'perfect' and 'ideal' are, one does not need to talk about dignity).

Friedrich Schiller, Goethe's and Kant's contemporary, has a broad understanding of dignity similar to Grossman's. In 'Die Künstler' (The Artists), one of his most famous poems, he refers to the dignity of humankind and demands that we all protect it. In this regard, he comes very close to Kant and also very close to the German constitution, which demands that dignity be protected.

Der Menschheit Würde	The dignity of Man,
ist in eure Hand gegeben,	into your hands is given
Bewahret sie!	Protector be!
Sie sinkt mit euch!	It sinks with you!
Mit euch wird sie sich heben!	With you it is arisen! (Schiller n.d.)

Hence, literary fiction and poetry also make broad reference to dignity, Grossman and Schiller being examples. But while it could be maintained that the earlier examples of dignity give the reader some information about what it is, the later examples leave the content blank. Schiller demands that we should all protect humankind's dignity, without indicating what it actually is. And Grossman chooses to equate all that is perfect with all that is dignified, leaving unclear why he thinks so and what this would add to the concept of dignity.

Of course, one cannot generalise *strong* claims from the above examples, few as they are. But it is nevertheless significant that in these selected novels and poems the use of dignity points towards it being a personal characteristic, and that the broader use of dignity in selected fiction tends to be vague.

If the foreign visitor who was invoked above were also to judge the football example, she would probably frown and ask how two people (the German and French journalists) could use the same term, 'dignity', to describe complete opposites. One of the journalists believed that Zidane had lost his dignity by attacking his Italian colleague, the other that he had kept and defended it. Matters would be complicated further if the visitor came across other quotes from the people mentioned above. For instance, Nelson Mandela said the following in an address to the South African parliament to mark ten years of democracy in 2004: 'We accord persons dignity by assuming that they are good' (Mandela 2004). This seems to contradict his earlier quoted view that the affluent must never fail to respond to the cries of the poor for food, shelter and dignity. If dignity were equated with being good, poverty cannot take this away or, in fact, make any difference.[6]

It seems that we have not progressed much in finding answers to the two riddles, which are, of course, related. The first riddle asks why something that is inviolable needs to be protected. This presupposes that human dignity is universal and therefore an intrinsic part of human beings. The second riddle asks whether dignity

---

[6]Moral luck and potential exceptions to this statement will not be dealt with here, as this chapter is confined to a general overview.

is indeed intrinsic to human beings, or whether one has to strive to achieve it. The next chapter will provide a brisk walk through philosophical history related to the concept of dignity and thereby also illuminate the origins of the two riddles.

2.3   A Very Short History of Dignity

> In early modern Europe, different 'dignities' marked off different levels of aristocrat from each other, and dignity separated all aristocrats from all the plain and ordinary people who altogether lacked dignity.
>
> Wood (2008: 48)

In pre-modern times the word 'dignity' referred to stratified societies in which some people were valued more highly than others. The German word *Würdenträger* (carrier of dignity, dignitary) clearly reflects these traditions. Carriers of dignity were invested with secular or religious positions of high rank, and they behaved in a dignified manner when acting in accordance with those positions. Often it was assumed that God invested carriers of dignity with their rank or that it was handed down through noble families. Kings, popes and other nobles would be regarded as dignified if their conduct befitted those of high rank (Beyleveld and Brownsword 2001: 58). Thus, dignity was restricted to an infinitesimally small number of human beings and strongly associated with their hierarchical position. Early in the concept's history, therefore, our two dignity riddles did not exist. Neither was dignity inviolable—carriers of dignity could lose their ranks, for instance, by losing wars— nor was dignity a universal feature.

Two prominent thinkers whose understanding of dignity was very much rank-related were Niccolò Machiavelli and Jeremy Bentham. In 1523, Machiavelli wrote:

> I answer that the principalities of which one has record are found to be governed in two different ways; either by a prince, with a body of servants, who assist him to govern the kingdom as ministers by his favour and permission; or by a prince and barons, who hold that dignity by antiquity of blood and not by the grace of the prince. (Machiavelli 2015)

In 1823, Bentham wrote:

> In order to obtain a post of rank and dignity, and thereby to increase the respects paid you by the public, you bribe the electors who are to confer it, or the judge before whom the title to it is in dispute. (Bentham 1831)

In Western philosophy, two of the earliest thinkers who moved the concept of dignity away from positions of high rank and hierarchies were Cicero (106–43 BC) and Pico della Mirandola (1463–1494). In *De Officiis*, Cicero makes an eloquent plea for dignity of character, a character 'free from every disturbing emotion, not only from desire and fear, but also from excessive pain and pleasure, and from anger'. Such control of emotions, he says, will lead to 'that calm of soul and freedom from care which bring both moral stability and dignity of character', and

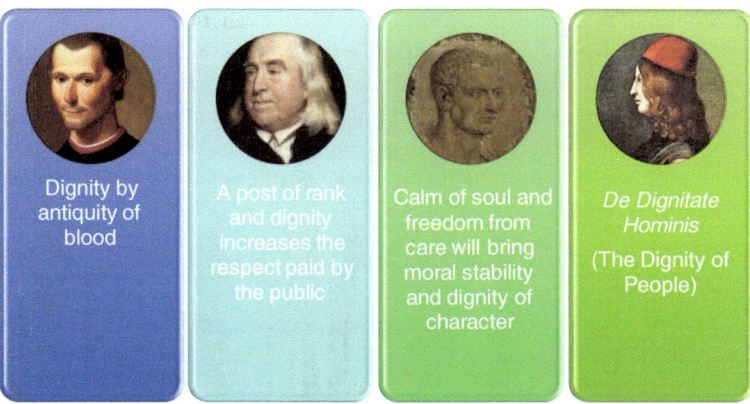

Fig. 2.4 Philosophers on dignity

that 'sensual pleasure is quite unworthy of the dignity of man' (Cicero 1913). In this regard, Cicero believes, with Goethe, that dignity can be achieved through effort. The fictitious childless couple and the poet who lost his daughter would be examples of people who controlled their emotions to achieve calm and dignity of character, despite their pain.

Some 1500 years later, Pico della Mirandola, an Italian Renaissance philosopher, wrote a pamphlet entitled *De Dignitate Hominis* (English title: Oration on the Dignity of Man) (Pico della Mirandola 2012). From the title alone, one can infer that Mirandola sees dignity as an attribute of human beings in general, rather than a rank. For Michael Rosen, dignity, in Mirandola's work, 'goes from being a matter of the elevated status of a few persons in a particular society to being a feature of human beings in general, closely connected with their capacity for self-determination' (Rosen 2012: 15). Mirandola paved the way for the philosopher who has most influenced dignity debates in the West, Immanuel Kant (Fig. 2.4).

2.3.1   Immanuel Kant's Concept of Dignity

Kant is widely regarded as the greatest Western philosopher in post-medieval times, if only because he is the only philosopher since Plato and Aristotle whom all others are expected to have read (Roberts 1988: 9). Given his role in defining dignity as an inviolable characteristic of human beings, it is worth looking at his philosophy in a little more detail.

Kant was not a preacher who developed his own moral code, but a thinker who believed that most human beings had the ability to distinguish good from bad actions intuitively. What he aimed to add with his philosophical work was a proof that a supreme law of morality (Kant 1997: 5 [4:392]) could be deduced from moral common sense. One of his most important thoughts was that 'it is impossible to think of anything at all in the world, or indeed even beyond it, that could be considered good without limitation except a good will' (Kant 1997: 7 [4:393]).

What does this mean? It means that to distinguish a moral action from an amoral or immoral one, one cannot rely on judging outcomes, but has to focus on intentions and motives instead. For example, a person gives a substantial sum to charity. Common moral sense would make a clear distinction between the following motives for the donation:

1. The donor intends to conquer the heart of a loved one with this generous gesture.
2. The donor hopes that her contribution will secure a position for her nephew in the administration of the charity.
3. The donor was moved to tears by a TV advertisement asking for donations and immediately transferred money into the charity's account.
4. The donor wanted to play her part in redressing injustice in the world.
5. The donor misread the instructions for an e-banking transaction and transferred money into the charity's account by mistake.

These actions seem to fall naturally into a moral hierarchy. Action 5, transfer by mistake, is morally neutral. Actions 1 and 2, with their hidden agendas, are morally deficient, action 2 probably more so than action 1. Actions 3 and 4 are both morally praiseworthy, but one's upbringing and moral judgements would determine which one a person would deem more worthy.[7] For instance, those who believe that empathy and compassion are the essence of morality, like David Hume (1711–1776) and Arthur Schopenhauer (1788–1860), would rate action 3 more highly. Kant himself would favour action 4.

How do human beings judge between good and bad actions? They require the human faculty of reason. Only because human beings are rational is it possible for them to be moral, to decide between right and wrong. This human ability to be rational and to make decisions is the basis for their dignity, according to Kant. Human beings have an 'unconditional and incomparable worth that unlike a price admits of no equivalence'; they have dignity (Hill 1992: 202–203). Or as Kant says:

> [A] human being regarded as a person, that is, as the subject of a morally practical reason, is exalted above any price; for as a person … he is not to be valued merely as a means to the ends of others or even to his own ends, but as an end in himself, that is, he possesses a dignity (an absolute inner worth) by which he exacts respect for himself from all other beings in the world. He can measure himself with every other being of this kind and value himself on a footing equal to them. … Humanity in his person is the object of the respect which he can demand from every other human being (Kant 1996, 6:434 ff).

Why do human beings have absolute inner worth (*absoluten innern Wert*) (Kant 1990: 74 [435])—in other words, dignity? Because of humanity's 'rational nature in its capacity to be morally self-legislative' (Wood 1999: 115). Thanks to their

---

[7]For an excellent summary of Hume's and Schopenhauer's 'ethics of sympathy' (*Mitleidsethik*), see Tugendhat (1993: 177–196).

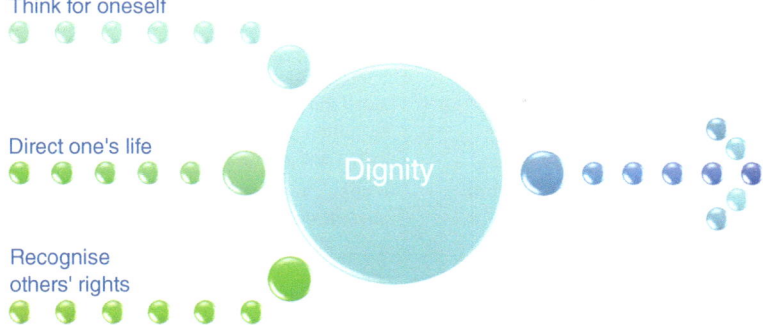

Fig. 2.5 Kant's concept of dignity according to Allen Wood

capacity for reason, human beings can establish and justify their own moral laws. They can ponder on whether it is morally right to lie in order to obtain a loan,[8] and they can come to the conclusion that it is not. This conclusion is open to all rational humans; humans can think and give themselves moral commandments. They are autonomous and, according to Kant, 'Autonomy is ... the ground of the dignity of human nature and of every rational nature' (Kant 1997: 43 [4:436]). Allen Wood paraphrases this idea of Kant's in the following, more accessible, manner (Fig. 2.5):

> We could sum up the qualities Kant thinks make for dignity if we said that dignity belongs to the capacity to think for oneself and direct one's own life with responsibility both for one's own well-being and for the way one's actions affect the rights and welfare of others. (Wood 2008: 54)

Surprisingly, dignity was not a term used often in philosophy before Kant (with the exception of Cicero and Mirandola). For instance, neither Plato nor Aristotle discussed the term. In legal debates, the concept's prominence was delayed even further.

2.3.2   Dignity in Legal Instruments

The term 'dignity' was not part of the language of law or jurisprudence before the 20th century. It was first mentioned in the constitution of the Weimar Republic in 1919, followed by the Portuguese constitution in 1933 and the Irish constitution in 1937 (Tiedemann 2006: 13). However, it was the concept's inclusion in international legal documents that marked its ascendancy. Table 2.2 lists some major legal instruments which make prominent reference to dignity, starting with the Universal Declaration of Human Rights in 1948.

The term 'human dignity' is present in constitutions around the world, including the Middle East, as the constitutions of Iran and Saudi Arabia show. However, the

---

[8]For more on this standard Kantian example, see below.

Table 2.2 Dignity in legal instruments and guidelines

Origin	Quote
UN Universal Declaration of Human Rights, 1948 (UN 1948: preamble)	… recognition of the inherent dignity and of the equal and inalienable rights of all members of the human family is the foundation of freedom, justice and peace in the world …
International Covenant on Civil and Political Rights, 1966 (UN 1966: preamble)	Recognizing that these rights derive from the inherent dignity of the human person …
Treaty on European Union (EU 2008: art. 2, art. 21)	The Union is founded on the values of respect for human dignity, freedom, democracy, equality, the rule of law and respect for human rights, including the rights of persons belonging to minorities The Union's action on the international scene shall be guided by the principles which have inspired its own creation, … [including] respect for human dignity
German constitution, 1949 (Germany 1949: art. 1, DS translation)	Human dignity is inviolable
Indian constitution, 1949 (India 2015: preamble)	We, the people of India, having solemnly resolved to constitute India into a Sovereign Socialist Secular Democratic Republic and to secure to all its citizens: justice … liberty… equality … to promote among them all fraternity assuring the dignity of the individual and the unity and integrity of the Nation …
Iranian constitution, 1979 (Iran 1979: art. 22)	The dignity, life, property, rights, residence, and occupation of the individual are inviolate, except in cases sanctioned by law
Saudi Arabian constitution, 1992 (Saudi Arabia 1992: art. 39)	Mass media and all other vehicles of expression shall employ civil and polite language, contribute towards the education of the nation and strengthen unity. It is prohibited to commit acts leading to disorder and division, affecting the security of the state and its public relations, or undermining human dignity and rights. Details shall be specified in the Law
Russian constitution, 1993 (Russia 1993: art. 7)	The Russian federation shall be a social state, whose policies shall be aimed at creating conditions, which ensure a dignified life and free development of man
South African constitution, 1996 (South Africa 1996: art. 1)	The Republic of South Africa is one, sovereign, democratic state founded on … [h]uman dignity, the achievement of equality and the advancement of human rights and freedoms

Iranian constitution does not regard human dignity as inviolable, as it can be overridden in cases sanctioned by law. The Saudi Arabian constitution mentions dignity only in the context of privacy rights, prohibiting all dignity violations by the media and other vehicles of expression. It does not mention dignity violations by the government or other forces.

Whether the concept of dignity is cited in the legal rulings of a country seems to be independent of whether it is included in the constitution concerned. For instance, the Canadian Supreme Court decided in 2008 that dignity was not to be used in anti-discrimination cases any longer as it was 'confusing and difficult to apply'.[9] By contrast, German courts use the concept frequently. A famous example is described in Box 2.1.[10]

Box 2.1 The Daschner case, Germany

On 27 September 2002, 11-year-old Jakob von Metzler, a banker's son, was abducted on the way home from school to his parents' house in Frankfurt, Germany. A large ransom was demanded and the alleged kidnapper, Magnus Gäfgen, was taken into custody following police observation. The case was discussed widely within Germany and abroad (Jenkins 2004), as Frankfurt deputy police chief Wolfgang Daschner threatened duress in order to obtain information regarding Jakob's whereabouts. At the time, Daschner assumed that Gäfgen might be a lone kidnapper and that Jakob might be dying of thirst in an unknown prison. However, Gäfgen had already killed Jakob (Der Mordfall Jakob von Metzler 2006).

In February 2003, Gäfgen was charged with abduction and murder. On 27 July 2003, he was found guilty of both, and sentenced to life imprisonment with no possibility of early release, due to the seriousness of the crime (Bourcarde 2004: 7f).

In February 2003, Daschner was charged with extortion of testimony by duress. In December 2004, a regional Frankfurt court ruled that Daschner had acted unlawfully. He was found guilty of the charge. In her summing up the chair of the court affirmed article 1 of the German constitution, which enshrines the inviolability of human dignity. She insisted: 'Human dignity is inviolable. Nobody must be made into an object, a bundle of fear' (Rückert 2004, DS translation). No human being may be treated as a mere carrier of knowledge that the state wants to access. According to the judges, Daschner lost his head under severe pressure and violated the principle of human dignity.

---

[9]R. v Kapp (2008) at para. 22: '[H]uman dignity is an abstract and subjective notion that … cannot only become confusing and difficult to apply; it has also proven to be an additional burden on equality claimants, rather than the philosophical enhancement it was intended to be.'

[10]For an excellent philosophical treatise on torture and scenarios like the one described in Box 2.1, see Brecher (2007).

One area that one cannot omit when presenting an overview of dignity discussions in the West is bioethics.

2.3.3   Dignity in Bioethics

The field of bioethics emerged in the 1960s in the wake of remarkable medical advances, such as organ transplantation, kidney dialysis, artificial respiration, contraception by pill and prenatal diagnosis. Simultaneously, people's consciences about the detrimental effects of technological advances on the environment were awakened, leading to the creation of green movements and parties. The possibilities that science was opening up were questioned, not only by environmental groups, but also increasingly by feminists. In this time of change, the field of bioethics was developed. According to Daniel Callahan, bioethics

> has come to denote not just a particular field of human inquiry – the intersection of ethics and the life sciences but also an academic discipline; a political force in medicine, biology, and environmental studies; and a cultural perspective of some consequence. ... Bioethics is a field that ranges from the anguished private and individual dilemmas faced by physicians or other healthcare workers at the bedside of a dying patient, to the terrible public and societal choices faced by citizens and legislators as they try to devise equitable health or environmental policies. (Callahan 1995)

The term 'dignity' achieved major prominence through two unconnected publications, both from the United States. One, known as *The Philosophers' Brief* (Dworkin et al. 1997), was written in the context of end-of-life decisions and used the concept positively. The other, written in the context of medical ethics and bioethics in general, rejected the use of the concept in those fields. This latter contribution from Macklin (2003) will be described in a separate, later section (see Sect. 2.5.2).

The Philosophers' Brief

In 1997, a group of highly eminent philosophers (Ronald Dworkin, Thomas Nagel, Robert Nozick, John Rawls, Thomas Scanlon, and Judith Jarvis Thomson) submitted a brief as *amici curiae* to the U.S. Supreme Court prior to its rulings on two physician-assisted suicide cases (see Boxes 2.2 and 2.3). In it they said:

> The Solicitor General concedes that 'a competent, terminally ill adult has a constitutionally cognizable liberty interest in avoiding the kind of suffering experienced by the plaintiffs in this case.' ... He agrees that this interest extends not only to avoiding pain, but to avoiding an existence the patient believes to be one of intolerable indignity or incapacity as well. (Dworkin et al. 1997)

The philosophers argued as follows:

> Most of us see death – whatever we think will follow it – as the final act of life's drama, and we want that last act to reflect our own convictions, those we have tried to live by, not the convictions of others forced on us in our most vulnerable moment.

Different people, of different religious and ethical beliefs, embrace very different convictions about which way of dying confirms and which contradicts the value of their lives. Some fight against death with every weapon their doctors can devise. Others will do nothing to hasten death even if they pray it will come soon. Still others, including the patient-plaintiffs in these cases, want to end their lives when they think that living on, in the only way they can, would disfigure rather than enhance the lives they had created. Some people make the latter choice not just to escape pain. Even if it were possible to eliminate all pain for a dying patient – and frequently that is not possible – that would not end or even much alleviate the anguish some would feel at remaining alive, but intubated, helpless, and often sedated near oblivion.

Box 2.2 State of Washington v. Glucksberg

Dr Harold Glucksberg (together with four other physicians and three terminally ill patients, as well as a not-for-profit organisation advocating physician assisted-suicide) brought a case again the State of Washington claiming that the ban on physician-assisted suicide was unconstitutional.

The case was decided unanimously in favour of the State of Washington.

The Court held that the right to assisted suicide is not a fundamental liberty interest … since its practice has been, and continues to be, offensive to our national traditions and practices. Moreover, employing a rationality test, the Court held that Washington's ban was rationally related to the state's legitimate interest in protecting medical ethics, shielding disabled and terminally ill people from prejudice which might encourage them to end their lives, and, above all, the preservation of human life. (Washington v. Glucksberg n.d.)

Box 2.3 Vacco v. Quill

Dr Timothy E Quill (together with other physicians and three seriously ill patients) brought a case against New York's attorney general Dennis Vacco, challenging the constitutionality of the New York State ban on physician-assisted suicide.

The case was decided unanimously in favour of Vacco and echoed some of the phrasing used in the earlier ruling.

Employing a rationality test …, the Court held that New York's ban was rationally related to the state's legitimate interest in protecting medical ethics, preventing euthanasia, shielding the disabled and terminally ill from prejudice which might encourage them to end their lives, and, above all, the preservation of human life. Moreover, while acknowledging the difficulty of its task, the Court distinguished between the refusal of lifesaving treatment and assisted suicide, by noting that the latter involves the criminal elements of causation and intent. No matter how noble a physician's motives may be, he may not deliberately cause, hasten, or aid a patient's death. (Vacco v. Quill n.d.)

While the courts in *State of Washington v. Glucksberg* and *Vacco v. Quill* decided against the plaintiffs, other cases brought on the basis of dignity have been granted.

In *Bouvia v. Superior Court* 28-year-old Elizabeth Bouvia sought a court order to remove her feeding tubes in order to allow her to die. Bouvia was quadriplegic, and had suffered from degenerative arthritis as well as severe cerebral palsy since birth. The court allowed the removal on the basis of her right to autonomy and thus her right to refuse lifesaving treatment:

> Here, if force fed, petitioner faces 15 to 20 years of a painful existence. ... Her condition is irreversible. ... Petitioner would have to be fed, cleaned, turned, bedded, toileted by others for 15 to 20 years! Although alert, bright, sensitive, perhaps even brave and feisty, she must lie immobile, unable to exist except through physical acts of others. Her mind and spirit may be free to take great flights but she herself is imprisoned and must lie physically helpless subject to the ignominy, embarrassment, humiliation and dehumanizing aspects created by her helplessness. (Vukadinovich and Krinsky 2001: 206)

Discussions of *The Philosophers' Brief* and the court rulings above often use the concept of dignity. The philosophers refer to 'intolerable indignity' which they go on to say involves being 'intubated, helpless, and often sedated near oblivion'. In their very graphic ruling on *Bouvia v. Superior Court*, the judges refer to situations that could be equated with indignity. However, as Shepherd (2012: 501) has aptly put it, it is one thing to accept a competent person's decision on the matter of life-sustaining treatment and quite another to dwell gratuitously on somebody's helplessness and toileting needs. 'Clearly the judges believe that a life such as Ms Bouvia's would be intolerable for them' (Shepherd 2012: 503). Instead of projecting their own ideas onto the case, they should have expressed an 'interest in or concern about the quality of care Ms Bouvia has received' (Shepherd 2012: 503). In fact, according to Shepherd, the court's assessment quoted above is 'so shockingly insensitive from any ethical standpoint that it does not take a French philosopher to point out its problems' (Shepherd 502).

As part of this short history of dignity discussions in the West, it is worth noting that there do not seem to be any major feminist theories of dignity. Lois Shepherd's emphasis on empathy and compassion in bioethics (as apparent from her commentary on the Bouvia case) has a feminist angle, but is not part of a feminist theory of dignity. The only exceptions seem to be articles, usually written by nursing scholars, which apply feminist theories to the problem of neglect of vulnerable individuals in health care (Aranda and Jones 2010).

The remainder of this chapter will attempt to disambiguate different concepts of dignity in the West. But first, one needs to ask whether dignity in legal instruments and bioethics can contribute to solving the two riddles.

Riddle 1: Why would something that is inviolable need protection?

Riddle 2: Is dignity merited, requiring constant effort, or is it intrinsic to human beings?

Riddle 1 can only be solved if the terms are changed. In contrast to the Iranian and Saudi Arabian constitutions, the German constitution wants to say that human dignity *should always* be inviolable. The emphasis is on both 'always' and 'should'. No factors or exceptions override the upholding of human dignity in all cases. As shown in the Daschner case, not even the life of a child can override the right not to be put under duress by the state. Hence, dignity *is not* inviolable but *should always be* inviolable. The judge presiding over the Daschner case insisted: 'Human dignity is inviolable. Nobody must be made into an object, a bundle of fear' (Rückert 2004, DS translation). She should have said that human dignity *should* be inviolable, not that it *is* inviolable, especially since she goes on to give an example of a dignity violation (the threat of torture and duress). If dignity were inviolable, no such example could be given. Hence, it is clear that the pronouncement of dignity as an allegedly inviolable attribute of human beings relies on legal protection, which explains why the German constitution starts with two statements, namely that 'human dignity is inviolable' and—importantly—that 'its protection is the duty of all state powers' (Germany 1949: art. 1 I, DS translation).

The second dignity riddle is more difficult to resolve, as it is about more than a legal contract or agreement. It is here that the disambiguation of different concepts of dignity is most important.

2.4   Disambiguating the Main Concepts of Dignity

So many roads, so much at stake

So many dead ends, I'm at the edge of the lake

Sometimes I wonder what it's gonna take

To find dignity

Dylan (1991)

One response to Bob Dylan's quest to find dignity would be to ask what he is looking for. An ideal and perfect world, a dignified world as David Grossman describes? A place where no state transgressions of torture or duress are allowed, as the ruling in the Daschner case required? A place where pain and disability are managed through empathic care and pain management, as might have been appropriate in the Bouvia case? A place where refugees are accepted without racism and based on considerations of historical fairness, as demanded by David McAllister, MEP? A place where nobody sleeps in public with their mouths lolling open, as Jonathan Coe's protagonist demands? It is clear from this short list that different concepts of dignity are at issue. We will attempt to disambiguate them, introducing new examples for emphasis. Before this, we lay a foundation for this disambiguation by asking what kind of concept dignity is.

2.4.1 What Kind of Concept Is Dignity?

A concept is an abstract idea, something one cannot touch or see or smell. It is a non-observable abstract entity. However, human beings can agree on the essence of concepts through language. An analogy with freedom might help clarify what kind of concept dignity is.

Nobody would claim that they can see, hear or smell freedom, but few would say that it cannot be explained or made intelligible to others. One could define freedom as the power to act or think without constraint or hindrance. Once one accepts this, or a similar definition, it is possible to experience violations of it with one's own senses. As soon as one understands the concept, one knows when it is violated.

For instance, sending somebody to prison violates their freedom of movement: they no longer have the power to act as they want to, for instance to go for a meal at the local Thai restaurant. Forcibly giving somebody hallucinogenic drugs violates their freedom of thought. It is contended that communicating what freedom of movement and freedom of thought require and knowing when those freedoms are violated are quite straightforward, even across cultural barriers. How does dignity fare by comparison?

Freedom and dignity are similar in some respects and different in others. The main similarity is that human freedom and human dignity need to be justified in a secular framework. Why should human beings have the power to act without constraint? Why should human beings have dignity and the consequent rights accorded through most modern constitutions? Answers to these questions cannot be taken for granted; justifications are required for both. However, in contrast to dignity, freedom can be broken down into smaller freedom packages: the freedom of movement, the freedom of choice and so on. These freedoms can be explained easily within and across cultural borders. If Ndugu Umbo, the little Tanzanian boy from the film *About Schmidt*, had wanted to travel to the United States to visit his sponsor, Warren Schmidt (played by Jack Nicholson), but failed to obtain a visa, his freedom of movement would have been restricted. People around the world would understand this explanation. Readers of Ray Bradbury's famous novel *Fahrenheit 451* readily understand that the systematic burning of books violates freedom of expression. If nobody can write down their thoughts and imaginings in books and have them preserved for others to read, they cannot be said to be free to express themselves.

Dignity, it seems, cannot so easily be broken into smaller dignity packages. For instance, as discussed above, Kant equates dignity with absolute inner worth. If one compares this explication of dignity with our short definition of freedom (the power to act without constraint), one sees that 'absolute inner worth' is simply a phrase equivalent in meaning to the word 'dignity'; it does not clarify what dignity is or implies. By contrast, 'the power to act without constraint' *explains* freedom. When one considers this explanation together with freedom's property of separability into individual parcels, in particular for purposes of illustration, it becomes clear why agreement on the meaning of 'freedom' can be achieved. Hence, if one accepts that 'dignity' and 'absolute inner worth' are no more than two different expressions of the same concept, one still needs a clarifying definition or explanation of what that concept means exactly. This task is tackled in the following sections, beginning with the question: is dignity a virtue?

2.4.2 Is Dignity a Virtue?

> Non-violence is the law of our species as violence is the law of the brute. The spirit lies dormant in the brute and he knows no law but that of physical might. The dignity of man requires obedience to a higher law – to the strength of the spirit.
>
> Gandhi (1920)

Earlier, a list of synonyms for 'dignity' was presented. They included 'correctness', 'graciousness', 'goodness', 'nobleness', 'restraint', 'pride' and 'reserve'. These could all be called virtues. Yet, to answer the question 'Is dignity a virtue?' one first needs an answer to the question 'What is a virtue?'

According to Solomon (2006: 91), 'virtues are cultivated responses and actions that may require no deliberation'. If somebody has to think too hard before acting virtuously, this may be an indication that the virtue concerned is not fully developed. For instance, if somebody with reasonable means takes weeks to decide whether to donate to an emergency charity appeal, pondering what else the money could buy or whether or not her donation is really necessary, she is not truly generous (generosity being a virtue). This aligns with Aristotle's belief that the test of virtue is enjoyment of a virtuous action. Those who always behave virtuously live life as it ought to be lived, according to Aristotle, and will enjoy *eudaimonia* (happiness) (Aristotle 2000: 5–19 [1095a–1101b]).

Philippa Foot, one of the founders of contemporary virtue ethics,[11] believes that

> virtues are … beneficial characteristics … that a human being needs to have, for his own sake and that of his fellows. … Nobody can get on well if he lacks courage, and does not have some measure of temperance and wisdom, while communities where justice … [is] lacking are apt to be wretched places to live … (Foot 1978: 3, 2)

This take on the virtues is again reminiscent of Aristotle and his belief that it is only the virtuous life that leads to human flourishing. Foot also emphasises another feature of virtue, which Aristotle noted in the *Nichomachean Ethics* (Aristotle 2000: 107 [1140b]): a virtue is different from a skill or an art (Foot 1978: 7). The difference between virtues on the one hand and skills or arts on the other can best be understood through the distinction of voluntary from involuntary error. If somebody is very good at spelling, but makes a deliberate mistake, which he later explains, his skill as a speller is not put into doubt. Yet if somebody acts unjustly and later claims that it was done deliberately, this is an even worse reflection on

---

[11]http://en.wikipedia.org/wiki/Philippa_Foot.

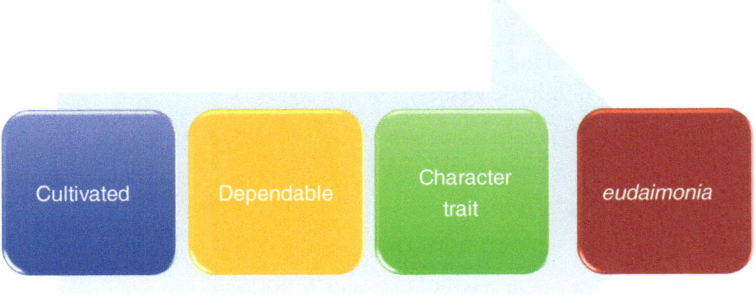

Fig. 2.6 Virtues

him. 'In the matter of arts and skills … voluntary error is preferable to involuntary error, while in the matter of virtues … it is the reverse' (Foot 1978: 7). A skill is unaffected by voluntary error, whereas a virtue disappears through voluntary error. Somebody who purposely undertakes an unjust action is simply not just.

If one possesses a virtue, one has not merely a moderate tendency towards a particular action, but a strong disposition towards it. For instance, if somebody is honest, one can reliably expect them to be so even under difficult circumstances. They will be honest, even if it is disadvantageous to them. They will value honesty in their friends and they will try to instil it in their children. Virtues, when present, are strongly entrenched, and to turn a genuinely honest man into a dishonest man or vice versa requires a profound change, for which one would normally expect some sort of unusual explanation (such as drugs or religious conversion) (Foot 1978: 11−14). One could therefore define virtues as follows (Fig. 2.6):

> Virtues are cultivated, dependable character traits, which human beings need in order to flourish.

Two of the literary examples of 'dignity' used at the outset fit the definition of 'virtue'. The couple that Iris Murdoch describes have achieved a quiet, though restrained, happiness despite the loss of a child. In his *Nichomachean Ethics*, Aristotle says: 'For the truly good and wise person, we believe, bears all the fortunes of life with dignity and always does the noblest thing in the circumstances' (Aristotle 2000: 18 [1101a]). Hence, Aristotle sees dignity in how one copes with life's accidents: to bear those with patience, courage and strength is the hallmark of dignity. The French writer whose story Paul Auster tells in *Oracle Night* bears a similar fate (losing a child) by resolving never to write again, carrying his suffering with fortitude.

A 2013 film from Germany, *Die Frau, die sich traut* (The Woman Who Dares) has a similar theme, and the film critic's summary refers to 'ethics and dignity'

(Hörzu 2015, DS translation). In the film, a former champion swimmer of the then German Democratic Republic discovers, at the age of 50, that she has terminal cancer as a consequence of doping. Instead of despairing, she reorganises her life for one last challenge, to realise her teenage dream of swimming across the English Channel. The way she copes with life's accidents and endures suffering with fortitude and strength is presumably what led the critic to use the term 'dignity'.

Dignity as a virtue fits the Goethe poem that is the basis of one of our riddles: 'A laurel is easier bound than a dignified head for it found.' One could also put the excerpt from the Dostoevsky novel in the category of dignity as virtue. It is his use of the term 'dignity' that makes his short description of two ladies who have fallen into poverty so evocative. It conjures up the image of quiet pride and resilience in the face of hardship, as well as a sense of preserved self-esteem, as noted earlier. While Dostoevsky does not speak of extreme poverty, as Mandela and Johnson do, it is noticeable that he sees dignity as a way of coping with poverty.

Another Russian author, Leo Tolstoy, elaborates his views on dignity in many of his novels. According to Clifton Fadiman,

> in Tolstoy's view evil and cruelty can never have dignity. Only the good man or he who strives for the good can have dignity. It follows then that no conqueror can have dignity. Someday the human race will learn this, and it will despise conquerors as it despises necrophiles. (Fadiman 1955: 198)

Examples that collaborate Tolstoy's view of dignity as a virtue can be drawn, again, from literature, politics, philosophy and everyday life.

In November 2015, the Ukrainian government stopped electricity supplies to the peninsula of Crimea, a region claimed by both Ukraine and Russia. In early January 2016, Ukrainian president Petro Poroshenko offered to restore power supplies on certain conditions. This is how the response of Crimeans was reported by Tass, the Russian news agency, quoting Irina Yarovaya, chairperson of Russia's State Duma security and anti-corruption committee:

> '… the Crimeans once again showed that they are Russians, the Russian people who never give up or sell out,' she said. 'Poroshenko's proposals falls into the category of obscene ones and the usual reaction to such thing is perfectly well known but Crimea answered "no" gently and with dignity.' …. [T]he data on a poll of residents of the Republic of Crimea … showed that 93.1% of those polled spoke against an agreement on purchases of electric power from Kiev if the latter document called Crimea and Sevastopol to be part of Ukraine. Also, 94% respondents said they were prepared to tolerate interim discomforts linked to short outages of electricity in the next three or four months if the electricity agreement with Ukraine was not signed. (TASS 2015)[12]

'Selling out' is a pejorative term for compromising one's integrity in return for personal gain (e.g. money). Thus refusing to sell out—in other words, tolerating discomfort to avoid compromising one's integrity—can be considered a virtue.

---

[12]This excerpt was chosen for its use of language. We cannot vouch for the accuracy or balance of its contents.

Nelson Mandela is frequently cited as a person with dignity. For instance, one of his biographers, Barry Denenberg, writes that Mandela's 'ability to conduct himself in a forceful yet dignified manner gradually won him the respect of the prison officials' (Denenberg 1995: 89). Called a man with 'breath-taking courage' and an 'almost messianic figure' (Crwys-Williams 1997: xii, xi), Beyleveld and Brownsword chose Mandela as an example of the personification of dignity, writing that 'if dignity is a virtue, it is found in the *character* of humans wrestling with the limitations of human finitude and the problems of social order' (Beyleveld and Brownsword 2001: 58). How Mandela dealt with his imprisonment, the fortitude displayed in the face of adversity, deserves almost universal admiration (Beyleveld and Brownsword 2001: 139).

From the above, one can conclude that there is at least one possible meaning of dignity that may be equated with virtue: the dignity to bear the accidents of life with poise. This would be one example of dignity as a cultivated, dependable character trait that human beings need in order to flourish—and, in some of the above cases, not to despair. It would also support Goethe in the dignity riddle. If dignity is a virtue, it cannot be a universal feature of humankind, as virtues need to be aspired to. Regarding dignity as a virtue therefore does cover some of the examples given so far, so one disambiguation was achieved, but more are necessary.

2.4.3   Is Dignity an Individual Characteristic not Covered by Virtues?

Certain individuals in the examples given from literature are characterised in detail through the use of the term 'dignity', but without reference to cultivated, dependable character traits. For instance, Olive Schreiner's heroine assumes 'the dignity of superior knowledge so universally affected by affianced and married women in discussing man's nature with their uncontracted sisters' (Schreiner 1989: 167). Sándor Márai's protagonist is reassured when told that his weight gain ('belly') means esteem: 'This comforted him, as he always endeavoured to exude dignity … to distract from his youth' (Márai 2005: 19f, DS translation).

Schreiner uses the term 'dignity' to describe the potentially pretentious feelings of superiority that married women have over their unmarried 'sisters'. She thereby uses the term to refer to a particular status that a group has achieved through its position rather than by cultivating a dependable, personal character trait. Throughout most of human history—and even today in many parts of the world —'wife of X' and/or 'mother of Y' was the most important position women could achieve on their own. Their consequent attitude of superiority towards unmarried women is emphasised through the terms 'assuming' and 'air of dignity'. Likewise Márai's use of 'dignity' seems to concern certain positions and the appearances necessary for them. The author describes a Hungarian gentleman who was pro-moted to a position in the 'central office' and has since aged prematurely, with signs of grey hair and midlife weight increase. These signs are interpreted as indicating dignity, which links dignity for men with age and the positions they can attain in midlife. Jonathan Coe is also concerned with appearances, but not with rank. His character's disapproval of sleeping in public is independent of *who* sleeps thus.

Before further examples are provided it will be helpful to understand Jean-Paul Sartre's concept of the gaze, which he describes as follows:

> The Other is the indispensable mediator between myself and me. By the mere appearance of the Other, I am put in the position of passing judgement on myself as an object, for it is as an object that I appear to the other. (Sartre 1958: 222)

What does it mean for the concept of dignity that the gaze of others turns us into objects, judged by them and by ourselves? The gaze is reminiscent of Jonathan Coe's traveller, who judges his fellow passengers on the train to be undignified. If dignity is inviolable, a property of human beings attached to them intrinsically and without external reference, as the first dignity riddle assumes, the gaze of others has no relevance. It is only when dignity is *bestowed* that others become important. Such dignity is meaningless for Robinson Crusoe, for example, assuming he will never re-enter human society. To be invested with such dignity requires at least one other person, which Robinson Crusoe does not have until Man Friday arrives.

In the examples given above that are role-related, the expectation of the gaze is dependent on the role. Jeremy Waldron explains that:

> Dignity ... was once tight up with rank: the dignity of a king was not the same as the dignity of a bishop and neither of them was the same as the dignity of a professor. (Waldron 2015: 12)

The dignity of a married woman or of a recently promoted office worker is not the same as the dignity of a schoolgirl or an apprentice. Bringing the two (the roles and the gaze) together, one could argue that it is acceptable to switch dignified conduct on and off as appropriate to the relevant roles. If a priest who solemnly leads a funeral procession during the day puts a tea cosy on his head and leaps around giggling at night, this need not be incompatible with the requirement that he show dignity as an incumbent of the priest's role.

In the case of Jonathan Coe's traveller, roles are irrelevant; only the presence or absence of onlookers is important. Going back to Thesaurus equivalents of dignity, it is good manners and etiquette that fit with Coe's protagonist's dismay at those sleeping in public. Societies have myriad rules about dignified comportment, and the protagonist in Coe's novel strongly believes that sleeping in public with one's mouth open and head lolling violates at least one of them. This example therefore relates directly to society's expectations of good manners and comportment. In the same way as Coe's protagonist believes it is undignified to sleep on the train, it could appear undignified to tell a rude joke at an official dinner with one's mouth full, to giggle at an obituary, to kiss one's beloved in a Catholic church (except at a specific point of the marriage ceremony, if one is the bride or groom), to spit onto the street, to undress or relieve oneself in public, to wear dirty clothes etc. Under normal circumstances, all of these are avoidable, the most important thing being, as with table manners, to know the local rules and to have the ability to fulfil one's basic needs (e.g. to have access to a bathroom and clean clothes). And as with role-specific dignity, comportment dignity depends upon the gaze of others. As Sartre put it, at its extreme: 'Nobody can be vulgar all alone!' (Sartre 1958: 222) To be offensive and rude (i.e. vulgar) requires a second person.

Individual people can thus be characterised further, using the term 'dignity', in two respects that are independent of virtues:

1. An individual's role-specific conduct can be described, which is linked to their rank and position.
2. An individual's compliance with rules of propriety and decency can be described. This is their comportment.

Further examples will clarify this distinction. The highly popular UK TV show *Strictly Come Dancing* sees celebrities learn to dance from professionals and perform their new skills in front of an audience and very critical judges. In 2010, a former minister of the UK government, Ann Widdecombe, took part. She says that when originally asked whether she would participate, she had 'replied with a horrified "No way!" I was still a serving politician. ... I'm retired now and need worry less about my dignity' (Widdecombe 2010). Ms Widdecombe was thus concerned about her rank- or position-specific dignity, not her personal dignity. As a serving politician, she did not want to take part in a dance competition, but as a retired politician she was happy to. To have dignity, in the sense of displaying dignified conduct in accordance with rank and position, requires an audience in a way that virtue does not. If the politician Ann Widdecombe had danced in her private home, on her own, that would not have endangered her dignity.

In the memoirs of Madame Germaine de Staël (1766–1817), a French intellectual, there is a description of her father, Jacques Necker, Louis XVI's minister of finance: 'He was rather silent, but made sly remarks and sharp repartees. He wrote several witty plays; but, thinking it beneath the dignity of a minister of State to publish them, he burnt them' (Child 1854: 18). Like Ann Widdecombe, Monsieur Necker did not object to an activity as such; he refrained from publishing plays on grounds of his dignity as a minister of state.

Going back to Mercier's *Night Train to Lisbon*, João Eça was worried that he had lost his dignity when he became incontinent. This is a common concern to the extent that a US company now markets its incontinence supplies as 'Dignity Incontinence Products'. The range includes Dignity Overnight Briefs and Dignity Comfort Underwear.[13] Another US company has developed a programme called Dignity Continence Solutions, which addresses the challenge of changing incontinence products regularly without excessively disturbing the incontinent person's sleep.[14]

---

[13]http://www.northshorecare.com/dignity-incontinence-products.html.
[14]http://hartmanndcs.com/.

Fig. 2.7 Aspirational dignity

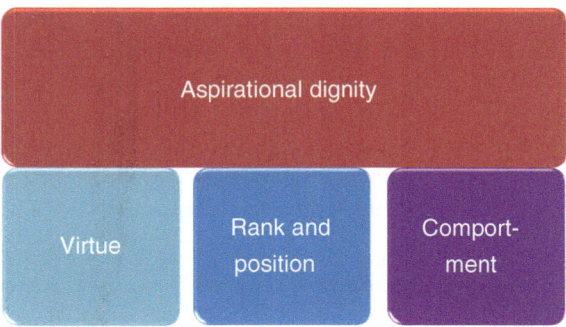

What these interpretations of dignity have in common is that they are contingent or aspirational.[15] Hence, the types of dignity they describe cannot be inviolable, as the first dignity riddle assumed, nor can they be intrinsic to human beings and never lost. They are varieties of dignity human beings aspire to: to be virtuous, to have superior rank or position and to conduct oneself appropriately when others are present.

We have therefore now disambiguated three meanings of dignity that are easily distinguishable. They all require effort, so one could class them all as aspirational dignity (Fig. 2.7).

Many of the examples given earlier do not qualify as aspirational dignity. In particular, the most famous Western dignity philosopher, Immanuel Kant, is not covered. Neither are religious sources, such as the Catholic church, as will be seen below.

2.4.4 Is Dignity Intrinsic to Human Beings?

Immanuel Kant argued that dignity is intrinsic to human beings due to their capacity for self-legislation—that is, their ability to think for themselves and to take responsibility for their own lives and well-being and those of others. To understand what kind of concept Kantian dignity is, one needs to ask what this means in practice.

2.4.4.1 Kantian Dignity Revisited

In the *Metaphysics of Morals*, Kant writes: 'He [the human being] possesses a dignity (an absolute inner worth) by which he commands (*abnötigen*) respect for

---

[15]While many philosophers use the term 'contingent dignity' to indicate the contrast with intrinsic dignity (see, for instance, Schaber 2012: 19), we use the term 'aspirational' here to emphasise the desirability of the features concerned: in other words, many humans aspire to displaying virtues or showing dignified comportment.

himself from all other rational beings in the world' (Kant 1990: 74f [435f], DS translation). Kant uses a very strong word in this context, 'command'. He thus wants the reader to focus strongly on the moral subject and their rights. A person with dignity is in the first place a right-holder. But what does it mean to be treated appropriately, as a being with dignity? The short answer to this is that one human being must not instrumentalise (i.e. [ab]use for one's own agenda) another human being without their reasonable[16] consent, or in Kant's own words:

> So act that you use humanity, whether in your own person or in the person of any other, always at the same time as an end, never merely as a means (Kant 1997: 38 [4:429]).

This statement of Kant's is also known as the *second categorical imperative* or the *Formula of Humanity* (Wood 1999: 111). If one follows this imperative, one respects the dignity of humanity through each individual action. Respecting human dignity is equivalent to 'always treat[ing] humanity, whether in your own person or in the person of any other, never simply as a means, but always at the same time as an end' (Kant 1997: 38 [4:429]). Lying, for instance—that is, making a promise one does not intend to keep—in order to obtain money is an example of disrespect for the dignity of humanity. The person who gives the money on the assumption that it will be returned in two weeks will have been used merely as a means rather than as an end; he or she will have been used for somebody else's agenda without consenting. And the person who lied

> ...wants to make use of another human being *merely as a means*, without the other at the same time containing in himself the end. For, he whom I want to use for my purposes by such a promise cannot possibly agree to my way of behaving toward him, and so himself contain the end of this action (Kant 1997: 39 [429–430]).

To contain the end of an action in oneself is Kant's way of saying that one is giving consent. If one agrees to an action, one carries the action's end in oneself. But liars do not reveal their true motives, they do not reveal their ends. Hence, it is not possible to consent to the 'real' action, as one is being deceived, used for another's purposes. And hence, dignity is an intrinsic and inviolable property of all rational beings, which gives the possessor the right never to be treated simply as a means, but always at the same time as an end.

That dignity is an intrinsic or inviolable property can be derived partly from Kant's claim that one cannot deny dignity even to a vicious man. At the same time, dignity is founded on the human ability to be self-legislative, and is therefore bound to rationality and restricted to rational beings. Kant's Formula of Humanity can then be used to provide content to the meaning or at least the implications of dignity. Can one be satisfied with these definitions? No, for two reasons.

First, what does it mean to treat a person never simply as a means, but always at the same time as an end? Explanations of abstract concepts should be clear and not require philosophical training to be understood, assuming one can understand them at all. In this context, W.D. Ross has noted that the Formula of Humanity only has

---

[16]Later (Sect. 2.4.4.4) I will explain why I have inserted the word 'reasonable' into this statement.

'homilectic value' (Ross 1969: 53), which means that it belongs to the art of preaching or that it is suitable for the art of sermonising to address the spiritual needs and capacities of a congregation. Similarly, Marcus Singer has noted that the Formula of Humanity 'has more an emotional uplift than a definite meaning' (Singer 1971: 236). Formulated slightly more positively, 'Kant's discussions of the second formulation contain both dross and gold' (Green 2001: 259). Clarifications are therefore necessary.

Second, why should dignity be an intrinsic or inviolable property? Freedom can be lost, so why can dignity not be lost? Even if one accepts that Kantian dignity is a concept wholly separate from the aspirational dignity described earlier, it is still unclear why all human beings should have this property. If human faculties to make reasoned moral decisions are the basis for dignity, what about those human beings who cannot make moral decisions because they lack rational abilities—such as toddlers, the severely mentally disabled, advanced Alzheimer's sufferers, patients in a persistent vegetative state? Do they have dignity and, if so, why?

2.4.4.2 The Meaning of the Formula of Humanity

What does it mean to treat another person or oneself never simply as a means, but always at the same time as an end? Literally thousands of scholars and teachers around the world have been trying to answer this question since the publication of Kant's *Groundwork of the Metaphysics of Morals* in 1785. Here is a brief selection of the most prominent ones.

Korsgaard (1998: xxiif) believes that never treating a person merely as a means equals respecting other people's rights to make their own decisions, implying particularly strong prohibitions on coercion and deception. This is so because both coercion and deception disable people's ability to make their own choices. The example that Kant uses in the *Groundwork*, which was mentioned before, is most instructive (Kant 1997: 32f [4:423]). Kant introduces his readers to a person who is suffering financial hardship; let us call him George. George considers borrowing money from a friend, knowing that he will not be able to pay it back. Hence, he will make a lying promise. In doing so, he is using his friend as a means to his own well-being only, without considering his friend as an end in himself, somebody with his own decisions to make. For instance, the friend may agree to lend George €1000—money he has set aside for his daughter's university tuition—for two months, on the assumption that it will be paid back promptly. By making a lying promise, George potentially wrecks his friend's plans without making him aware of this possibility. George thus instrumentalises or uses his friend for his own purposes.

Tugendhat (1993: 146) believes that never treating a person merely as a means equals respecting other people's purposes and ends. However, it would be absurd to insist that other people never be used as means to fulfil one's own ends. Buying flowers at the local garden shop implies using the shop assistant as a means to one's own aesthetic preferences. And why should this be forbidden? What is forbidden, in Kantian moral theory, is to use somebody *merely* as a means. In our example, the shop assistant presumably works willingly in the shop and is pleased when somebody comes to buy flowers. She therefore is likely to agree to such purchase transactions. But if she did not agree to the transaction, her purposes would not be respected. For instance, if the last flowers had already been sold and were awaiting collection, somebody who grabbed them, threw money onto the counter and ran out would be treating the shop assistant as a mere means to their own ends. This person would have instrumentalised somebody else for their own purposes.

Paton (1948) believes that treating a person merely as a means equals using them for the satisfaction of one's own inclinations without considering them as a person of unconditional and absolute value. Treating oneself merely as a means for one's own inclinations is apparent when one does not seek one's own perfection or the happiness of others. Paton's interpretation is demanding, in that it requires considerable altruism to promote other people's interests to achieve their happiness together with constant efforts at self-improvement. Kant himself did not assign significant moral force to the duty to secure the happiness of others.

Wood's (2008: 52) interpretation is worth quoting:

> I think a more immediate conclusion from the fact that humanity is an end in itself is that human beings should never be treated in a manner that degrades or humiliates them, should not be treated as inferior in status to others, or made subject to the arbitrary will of others, or be deprived of control over their own lives, or excluded from participation in the collective life of the human society to which they belong.

So what does it mean to treat another person or oneself never simply as a means, but always at the same time as an end? The answer of this co-author (DS) is that never treating a person merely as a means equals respecting their sense of purpose and their sense of self-worth, unless the person themselves violates this principle—for example, self-defence against an attack would be allowed. Not respecting somebody's sense of purpose means restricting their pursuit of life-plans. Not respecting their sense of self-worth means humiliating them. To add the proviso for self-defence and related issues, one could define never treating a person merely as a means as not restricting their *reasonable* pursuit of life-plans nor humiliating them (more below in Sect. 2.4.4.4) (Fig. 2.8).

2.4.4.3 Do All Human Beings Have Kantian Dignity?[17]

If rationality gives human beings dignity, what about those who have lost or have never had the faculty of rationality? Would it not mean that with the loss of rationality they also lose dignity, which therefore cannot be intrinsic or inviolable?

---

[17]If the question were 'Do all human beings have dignity?' we would respond with Peter Schaber that the question has to be answered separately for each concept of dignity (Schaber 2012: 13). The question here is whether Kantian dignity can be intrinsic to all human beings.

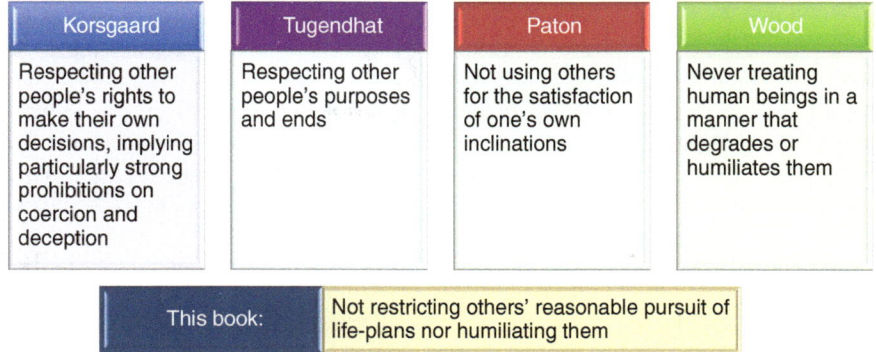

Fig. 2.8 Interpretations of the Formula of Humanity

According to Kant, 'the dignity of humanity consists in just this capability, to be universally legislating' (Kant 1997: 46 [4:440]). Ideally, all human beings would have this capability and therefore the entire species would be blessed with dignity. If this were the case, the only criterion needed for the conferment of dignity would be to be born of human parents. As soon as we saw a fellow human, we would see a carrier of dignity from birth to death. This is what the constitutions quoted previously (Table 2.2) suggest. But not all human beings have the capacity for rational decision-making and autonomy that Kant requires.

> Kant ... [insisted] that persons are ends in themselves with an absolute dignity who must always be respected. ... [But] while all normally functioning human beings possess the rational capacities that ground respect, there can be humans in whom these capacities are altogether absent and who therefore, on this view, are not persons. ... (Dillon 2014)

This would mean that the progression from rationality or autonomy to dignity works only for those who have rationality. This is how Kant scholar Thomas E. Hill Jr. interprets Kant when he writes: 'Kant attributes human dignity to virtually all sane adult human beings' (Hill 1991: 169)' If one's purpose is to confer obligations or rights on entities that have dignity, one has a problem, which Allen Wood describes as follows:

> No doubt some people are smarter or more rational than others in many respects. But less smart or less rational people, assuming they are responsible agents, are possessed of exactly the same dignity as smarter people. And every being with 'humanity' and 'personality' may be regarded as a co-legislator of the laws that are binding on the community of rational beings. So a morally bad person is just as much a person with dignity as a morally good person. There are complex questions regarding borderline cases of rational agency, or what some like to call 'nonideal conditions': for instance, how we should treat children, the mentally ill or people suffering from Alzheimer's disease. Kantian ethics, along with other views, must deal with these questions, but I will not pursue them here. One sort of answer *not* open to Kantian ethics, closed off by the very concept of human dignity, would be to treat persons as unequal, some having greater dignity than others. (Wood 2008: 54)

Wood maintains that as long as people are responsible agents, they have dignity. In this regard, he follows Kant. He also sees that there are complex questions to be answered about borderline cases of rational agency, questions he does not pursue himself. Yet, at the same time, he maintains that it is not open to Kantians to deny dignity to any human being, including those who are not responsible agents. If one maintained, in line with Kant's dictum, that dignity requires rationality, one could come to shocking conclusions about not applying the Formula of Humanity to toddlers, for instance.

However, the first point to be made here is that it does not follow that those who have no Kantian dignity can be mistreated. One would require a separate discussion of (a) the rights of those without dignity and (b) the obligations of rational beings towards those without dignity.

Furthermore, Kantians have considered possible ways out of this dilemma. The most radical move is to argue that species rationality (Wetlesen 1999) (*zôon logon*, *animale rationale*) confers dignity, independent of the reasoning faculties of individual human beings. The argument would then be that the human species is a species of rational beings and that all those who belong to the species should enjoy the benefits that are obtained through common species features. This move is conceptually rather unsatisfactory, as it confers a feature on a group on account of certain characteristics that only some of the group own. It is therefore an untenable ad hoc accreditation that takes for granted a certain outcome (we want all human beings to have dignity) and tries against the odds to find a secular, Kantian justification for it. In doing so, it loses the justification Kant himself gave, namely that rationality confers dignity. Singer (1995) has shown that what he refers to as speciesism (of which species rationality would be an instance) is not philosophically tenable. George Kateb has also noted that species references in the context of dignity are a backward step. He writes:

> The species, not the individual becomes the centre of thinking about human dignity, and we are threatened with being thrown back to earlier times before the concept of individual status had the central place or any place at all, and stature did practically all the work in dignifying and elevating human beings in their own eyes. (Kateb 2011: 211)[18]

The most common move to avoid the problem of excluding a large number of humans (e.g. all children) from the realm of dignity is to argue that 'potential rationality' confers dignity, not 'rationality' (Cohen 2001). This means that all those who are still developing the capacity of rationality (including children) or all those who have only lost it temporarily (e.g. those in a reversible coma) are included in the realm of dignity. If they were not, even people who are sleeping would have no Kantian dignity. Although Kant himself never pronounced judgement on the question, this would seem most counter-intuitive. Those who have a temporary lack of rational capacity must be included in the realm of dignity. However, those who have irrevocably lost the capacity to retrieve their rational faculties and thereby their

---

[18]Kateb makes this claim in the context of human beings' alleged superiority to all other living beings, not that of rationality.

ability for moral self-legislation cannot be included in the Kantian definition. As such dignity is not intrinsic or inviolable, even though the vast majority of human beings partake of it. This may be a deplorable result, but within the Kantian justification of dignity it is unavoidable. As Bontekoe puts it when writing about Kant's understanding of dignity:

> The difference between being fully human and being merely a human animal – and thus the difference between possessing and lacking the dignity attendant upon one's humanity is a matter of one's possessing autonomy, a matter of being a free initiator of events rather than a mere conduit for impulses provided one by nature. (Bontekoe 2008: 6)

Unusually for a virtue ethicist, Martha Nussbaum puts this even more strongly and argues that the one who is not able to shape her own life as a dignified free being and for whom 'the absence of capability for a central function is … acute … is not really a human being at all' (Nussbaum 2000: 73). Similarly, Dieter Birnbacher claims that 'human dignity in its "concrete" and strong form is a normative property only of those human beings who are capable of self-consciousness' (Birnbacher 1995: 9, DS translation).

This move closes the reasoning gap on why most human beings have the right always to command respect for their reasonable sense of purpose and self-worth. Persons—as Kant calls them, the subjects of a morally practical reason—are exalted above any price and possess an absolute inner worth—that is, dignity—because of their capacity for moral self-legislation. As a result, they have rights. While one can thus justify rights via dignity, one loses the attribution of dignity to *all* human beings. For those who cannot accept this, Paul Tiedemann argues that unwanted implications of reasoning chains do not invalidate the chain. He notes that the unwanted exclusion of some human beings from the dignity realm

> is no valid objection. The foundation of a concept cannot be dependent on wished-for results. Otherwise one does not provide a foundation, but instead utters more or less concrete … intuitions, whose justification remains open. (Tiedemann 2006: 111−112, DS translation)

Those who object to a reasoning chain for no reason other than its result exclude themselves from rational discussion (Tiedemann 2006: 112). However, this does not mean that Kantians would have nothing to say about those human beings who do not belong to the realm of rationality. Dignity is not the only available moral principle to inform obligations and rights. However, the right to have one's reasonable sense of purpose and self-worth respected only accrues to rational beings. One would therefore derive obligations towards non-rational beings differently. Since that is not the topic of this book, one brief example of a possible approach has to suffice.

One could reason along the lines of the first rather than the second categorical imperative: namely, to act only according to that maxim whereby you can at the same time will that it should become a universal law (Kant 1997: 14 [4:402]).

Simplified, the first categorical imperative is a refined version of the Golden Rule, 'Do unto others as you would have them do unto you.' But it is not so much a simple prescription that one can follow as a testing mechanism which can be applied prior to action. For instance, if one were to consider whether to lie during a job interview, one would need to ask whether the underlying maxim ('lie to get a job') could be universalised. What would happen if everybody lied to get a job? If this became a universal rule, interviews would no longer be conducted as the appointment committee would no longer be able to ascertain any meaningful information through the procedure. Kant is here specifically interested in the logical impossibility of universalising this maxim (if everybody lied in interviews, interviews would be abandoned altogether) rather than the non-desirability of the outcomes (e.g. if people lied to get jobs as doctors, that would endanger patients).

Applying the first categorical imperative can lead to what Kant calls contradictions in conception as well as contradictions of the will. A contradiction in conception means that the action, if universalised, would lead to the annulment of the basis for the action. In the above case, interviews would be abolished if everybody lied to get a job. Or if everybody robbed banks to get money, all banks would close, and as a result nobody could rob a bank. The basis for the action would be nullified.

Contradictions in will do not cause such severe complications, but cannot be willed by rational beings. For instance, one cannot will that all those with severe Alzheimer's should be left to die. Rational beings would not want to live in a world where the above maxim applied, partly because it might apply to themselves one day and partly because rationality, for Kant, is strongly linked with morality and therefore benevolence to others. But since severe Alzheimer's would not disappear even if this cruel maxim were realised, we have no contradiction of conception, but a contradiction of will.

While the above has argued that Kant could not extend dignity to all human beings, but only to all rational beings, a definition of dignity which is inclusive of all human beings can still exist in two separate ways. First, one could say that human dignity is a thought construct agreed upon by legitimate representatives of a country's peoples or even world leaders, which is then transformed into binding legislation. The existence of dignity would then have been agreed upon contractually for reasons of social utility, because this will lead to, for instance, a more peaceful society. And, of course, under such circumstances the legitimate representatives could agree that it applies to all human beings. It is an artefact, after all. However, this possibility faces obstacles. Usually dignity is given prominence in constitutional law and similar instruments as the foundation for detailed human rights. If dignity were a construct agreed upon by parliamentarians and then written into law to promote a more peaceful society, one might as well omit this step and agree the human rights directly. The reason dignity is so prominent—not only in law, but in literature, the media, politics and moral decision-making—is that many think it is not a mere thought construct.[19]

---

[19]Meir Dan-Cohen favours a social approach to dignity, which does not rely on Kantian metaphysics and *noumenal* selves. Dan-Cohen (2015: 8) argues that this approach could treat humanity as a biological species so that 'the extension of *Homo sapiens* is as naturally fixed as is the extension of *Loxodonta africana* [the African bush elephant]. *Who* is a human being is a given; *what* she is, is not.'

The alternative is to proclaim that dignity is God-given, and this belief has not lost its influence, even in an era when the authority of the Christian church—at least in many parts of the Western world—has waned. This will be recalled in the next section.

Before we add another disambiguation to the list of dignity meanings in terms of Kant's Formula of Humanity (always treat humanity never simply as a means, but always at the same time as an end), one loose end needs to be tidied up. The formula was explained in two ways, one formulated positively, the other negatively.

1. Human beings must *not* instrumentalise (i.e. use or abuse for one's own agenda) other human beings without their reasonable consent.
2. Human beings have the right always to command respect for their reasonable sense of purpose and self-worth.

What does 'reasonable consent' or 'reasonable sense of purpose' mean in this context, and why is it important? Answering this question will contribute to resolving the first dignity riddle, as we will see below.

2.4.4.4 Does Kant Protect the Sense of Purpose and Self-worth of a Criminal?

Does the respect for dignity inspired by the Formula of Humanity imply that one has to look at every single person's ends and purposes in one's moral actions? Does one have to treat others in accordance with their own purposes, determined by their own hopes, dreams, fears, and desires (Neumann 2000: 286)? After all, prominent philosophers such as Charles Taylor interpret Kant to mean that 'human dignity ... consist[s] largely in autonomy, that is, in the ability of each person to determine for himself or herself a view of the good life' (Taylor 1995: 245). This would mean that everybody's individual view of the good life is worthy of respect. In the words of Bjørn Hofmann, who interprets Kant similarly,

> individuals have to be taken into account as whole persons, and their particular conception of the good life and individual way of prospering and flourishing in it has to be acknowledged. That is, one has to attend to and respect the dignity (Hofmann 2002: 89).

This implies that human beings with their different ideas about a good life, in all their diversity, deserve respect as entities with dignity. Yet, this is *very far* from Kant's understanding of respect for human dignity, 'for the criminal would argue on this ground against the judge who sentenced him' (Kant 1997: 39 [4:430]). This is a dilemma, of course. The Formula of Humanity could enable criminals to argue that their sense of purpose and self-worth are being violated through, for instance, punishment. However, this is not at all in line with Kant's spirit.

In order to explain Kant's response to the criminal, Kant's distinction between the *noumenal* and the *phenomenal* world is important. The Greek words *noein* (to perceive through thought) and *nous* (mind) combine to form the term *noumenon*, an object or a world that cannot be perceived through the senses, but only through pure intellectual intuition. As humans are not capable of pure intellectual intuition (only God is, according to Kant) this world is sometimes thought of as an unknowable world, which cannot be proven. Kant also calls *noumenal* objects things in themselves (*Dinge an sich*). By contrast, the *phenomenal* world is the empirical world, which can be perceived and understood through the senses, the world as one sees it in time and space. The way objects present themselves is dependent on the perceiving mind. For Kant, God is entirely in the *noumenal* world, while animals only share in the *phenomenal* world. Human beings are part of both worlds: their rationality is part of the *noumenal* world, their bodies and their inclinations are part of the *phenomenal* world (Kant 1998).

Kant is not interested in humanity as comprising individual, highly diverse, empirical selves with their unique dreams, lives and purposes. These individual dreams and aspirations are part of the *phenomenal* world, which human beings share with animals. Kant is only interested in human beings as autonomous self-legislators and part of the *noumenal* world. As noted earlier, what gives human beings dignity, according to Kant, is their rationality, and it is this rationality that gives them access to the *noumenal* world (Fig. 2.9). As Neumann (2000: 286) aptly put it:

> When I contemplate how to treat you, I'm in no way guided by your natural inclinations, your hopes, desires or dreams. These are put to one side. They are unworthy of you as a *person*, a *homo noumenon*, and belong to you only as an intrinsically worthless thing, a *homo phaenomenon*. Treating your rational nature as an end in itself, I ask whether my actions towards you are consistent with the universal principles of pure practical reason. I ask whether my act could be a universal practice, and willed as such. Once I have done so, I'm through with my moral deliberation: if the act is universalizable, I perform it; otherwise not. No messy consideration of what you want as a flesh-and-blood human is required; indeed it is positively excluded.

As Neumann has explained, those parts of human beings that make us distinct flesh-and-blood creatures—perhaps artists, plumbers, novelists, lawyers or criminals—are not relevant to moral decision-making for Kant. One does not need to

Fig. 2.9 Kant's moral world view

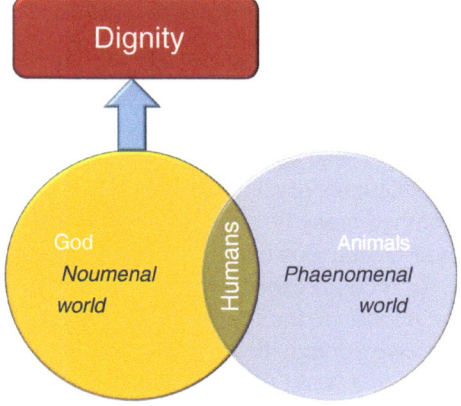

listen to and get to know another person in detail before being able to decide how to treat them. In one's dealings with other humans, it does not matter whether one is a woman from rural Nigeria and another a male from the capital of Sweden, with extraordinarily different life purposes. What matters is that the moral decision can be universalised across all human beings. For instance, since rational nature is an end in itself, in other words an entity with absolute inner worth, it is universalisable to prohibit the murder of humans. 'Do not kill' is therefore a universalisable moral precept. A woman from rural Nigeria cannot be stoned to death if she has committed adultery, and a man from Stockholm cannot be killed even if his liver would save the life of the pope. This leads to powerful demands, eloquently formulated by Allen Wood:

> The demand that we treat every human being with equal dignity would challenge most ideas, in most cultures, about how people ought to regard one another. … Human dignity is in this way very dangerous in that it threatens to undermine all traditional ways of life in all cultures. (Wood 2008: 62)

When Kant's thoughts on dignity were first quoted from the *Metaphysics of Morals,* one technical term (used in brackets by Kant) was left out. Now the quote in full.

> [A] human being regarded as a person, that is, as the subject of a morally practical reason, is exalted above any price; for as a person (*homo noumenon*) he is not to be valued merely as a means to the ends of others or even to his own ends, but as an end in himself, that is, he possesses a dignity (an absolute inner worth) by which he exacts respect for himself from all other beings in the world. (Kant 1996: 144 [6:434ff])

Kant does not ask for respect for flesh and blood humans. He asks for respect for the part of humans that belongs to the *noumenal* world. Before proceeding to his view on dignity, Kant writes:

> [I]n the system of nature, a human being (*homo phaenomenon, animal rationale*) is a being of slight importance and shares with the rest of the animals, as offspring of the earth, an ordinary value (*pretium vulgare*). Although a human being has, in his understanding, something more than they and can set himself ends, even this gives him only an extrinsic value for his usefulness (*pretium usus*); that is to say, it gives one man a higher value than another, that is, a price as of a commodity in exchange with these animals and things, though he still has a lower value than the universal medium of exchange, money, the value of which can therefore be called preeminent (*pretium eminens*). (Kant 1996: 144 [6:434ff])

It is only through sharing in the world of rationality, of pure intellect, the *noumenal* world, that human beings are raised beyond ordinary value. This shows again that Kant did not think of dignity as independent of rationality. Only rational beings have dignity. It is now also clear what Kant would say to criminals. Criminals are dominated by their inclinations and desires, which are part of the *phenomenal* world. Had they been guided by reason rather than inclination, they would not have committed a crime. This explanation of the Formula of Humanity, which captures its Kantian spirit appropriately, might seem austere. However, for Kant, 'autonomy lies in the power to act on the basis of duty rather than inclination, whereas in American culture, with its strong libertarian streak, it means the power

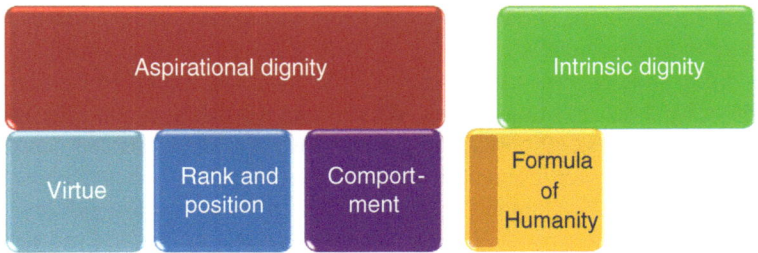

Fig. 2.10 Aspirational and intrinsic dignity I

of acting on inclination rather than duty' (Luban 2005: 826). To understand autonomy as the freedom of individuals to do and to be whatever they like, and human dignity as ensuring that this pursuit of life purposes remains sacrosanct, is to misunderstand Kant significantly (Hayry 2005: 645). Respect is not due to the part of human beings that is influenced by inclinations.

For the reasons given above, the term 'reasonable' (based on rationality, as part of the *noumenal* world, to use Kantian terms) was added to the clarifications of the Formula of Humanity, which we can now add as a separate disambiguation to the dignity categories (Fig. 2.10). The contribution of this move to the first dignity riddle will be spelled out in the conclusion of the Western dignity section, but we first need to return to the claim that dignity is intrinsic to all human beings, not only rational human beings, because it is God-given.

2.4.5 Is Dignity God-Given? the Example of Christianity

Religion and dignity will be examined in more detail in the section that analyses the concept in the context of Islam. However, a section on dignity in the West would be incomplete without reference to the Christian understanding of dignity. Given that many prominent pronouncements on the topic come from Catholic popes and that Catholicism is the oldest of the main Christian denominations, this section will focus on Catholicism. The Catholic understanding is also of interest because it covers all humans beings in a way that Kantian dignity does not, as was seen above.

For Catholics as Christians, dignity derives from God and the belief that human beings are formed in his image. The director of the Centre for Clinical Ethics in Toronto, an institution established by the Catholic Church, Hazel Markwell, describes this as follows:

> The value of dignity of the individual arises from the belief that life has intrinsic worth because people are created in the image and likeness of God. (Markwell 2005: 1132)

Commenting on care for patients in a persistent vegetative state (who would be excluded from a Kantian dignity definition), the Archbishop of Philadelphia, Cardinal Justin Rigali, and Bishop William Lori say:

> Our love and support for patients in P.V.S. should be modelled on God's love, which is
> based not on their current ability to act and respond but on their enduring dignity as human
> beings, made in his image and likeness and facing an ultimate destiny with him. (Rigali and
> Lori 2008: 15)

For theologian Ulrich Eibach, the 'character of an "image" implies that God has
created and chosen man as his partner' (Eibach 2008: 68). The Christian anthro-
pology of humans as created in the image of God is prominent, as the quotes above
show. It has been expressed by Pope John Paul II as follows:

> 'Man, living man, is the glory of God.' Man has been given a sublime dignity, based on the
> intimate bond which unites him to his Creator: in man there shines forth a reflection of God
> himself. (John Paul II 1995)

In some Christian texts, human dignity is regarded as God-given primarily
because humans are created in the image of God, but also because of Jesus' human
sacrifice. Bishop James McHugh (2001: 441) says: 'Human dignity derives from
God's creation of each person, redemption of Jesus Christ, and the call to eternal
happiness'. De Chirico (2005: 255) believes that 'Jesus' assumption of human
nature elevates man to 'divine dignity''. The Bishops of Texas and the Texas
Conference of Catholic Health Facilities (2006: 190) explain very clearly that '[t]he
life of each person has an inherent dignity. ... Each person is of incalculable worth
because all humans are made in the image of God, redeemed by Christ'.

For practising Catholics, dignity therefore needs no other justification. It is
God-given to all and does not require Kantian foundations such as the capacity for
moral self-legislation. Hence, dignity is an intrinsic and inviolable property that
God invests in *all* human beings. But as with Kantian dignity, it is important to
examine what Catholic dignity actually means. In the Kantian example, the
Formula of Humanity was helpful. We will now attempt to clarify the meaning of
Catholic dignity by examining what violates such dignity.

Patrick Lee, a Catholic professor of bioethics, argues that 'suicide [is...] contrary
to the intrinsic dignity of human persons' (Lee 2001). Presbyterian minister and
bioethicist Holly Vautier maintains that the 'dignity of all human life has been
influential in maintaining ... prohibitions against abortion' (Vautier 1996). Pope
John Paul II declares that even '[t]he sick person in a vegetative state ... still has the
right to basic health care ... even when provided by artificial means' (John Paul II
2004).

From the above prohibitions against suicide and abortion, and the equation of
artificial means of health care with the right to basic health care, one can assume
that God-given dignity makes human life sacred. If dignity forbids suicide, abortion
and the removal of feeding tubes, then dignity demands respect for the sanctity of
human life. This claim can be corroborated further by the following quotations.

It has been argued that Pope John Paul II identified 'new threats to the dignity of
the human person. A new cultural climate is developing which gives attacks on, and
threats to, human life a new and more sinister character' (McHugh 2001: 442). Here

the author clearly equates a threat to human dignity with a threat to human life. When Hazel Markwell discusses God-given human dignity, as noted above, she refers to the intrinsic worth of human beings because of their likeness to God. She follows this description of human dignity as God-given with the claim that 'respect for human life results from this principle' and that 'life is said to be sacred' (Markwell 2005: 1132). The Bishops of Texas and the Texas Conference of Catholic Health Facilities (2006: 190) also claim that 'each person, regardless of age or condition, has exactly the same basic right to life'.

The link between dignity and the sanctity of life is most clearly expressed in Pope John Paul II's *The Gospel of Life*, the encyclical issued in 1995:

> [T]he Gospel of the dignity of the person and the Gospel of life are a single and indivisible Gospel. (John Paul II 1995)

He also writes that 'every murder is a violation of the "spiritual" kinship uniting mankind in one great family, in which all share the same fundamental good: equal personal dignity' (John Paul II 1995). Commenting on abortion, he asks: 'How is it still possible to speak of the dignity of every human person when the killing of the weakest and most innocent is permitted?' (John Paul II 1995).

Pope Francis agrees. In an address to the US Congress in September 2015, he condemned the death penalty and demanded its global abolition.

> I am convinced that this way is the best, since every life is sacred, every human person is endowed with an inalienable dignity. ... (Francis 2015)

In Catholic belief, dignity and the sanctity of life are therefore inseparably linked. In fact one could say that the sacredness of life is the equivalent of the Kantian second categorical imperative. It lays the foundation for duties and rights with regard to human beings. This means that we now have two types of intrinsic dignity: the Kantian sense that applies to all rational beings and argues that they have inalienable rights never to be treated as mere means of somebody else's ends, and the Catholic belief that the intrinsic dignity of all human beings can be equated with the sanctity of human life (Fig. 2.11).

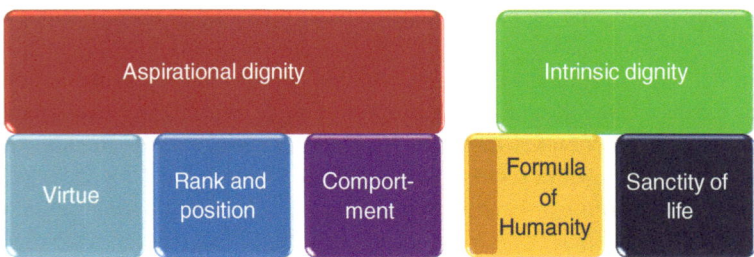

Fig. 2.11 Aspirational dignity and intrinsic dignity II

2.5 Testing and Critiquing the Taxonomy of Dignity

Discussions have so far elicited a distinction between aspirational and intrinsic dignity, each of which has further elements. The preceding section presented a range of examples. These and a few additional final examples will now be used to test this taxonomy of dignity in the West. Is it clear? Is it comprehensive? Can new examples be grouped under the five headings set out in Fig. 2.11?

In 2008, the National Union of Journalists in the United Kingdom published *Stop Bullying: Challenging Bullies and Achieving Dignity at Work* (NUJ 2008). The document describes procedures to stop bullying interchangeably as 'harassment' or 'dignity at work' procedure (NUJ 2008: 16). The report defines harassment as:

> Unwanted conduct affecting the dignity of men and women in the work place. It may be related to age, sex, race, disability, religion, nationality, sexual orientation or any personal characteristic of the individual, and may be persistent or an isolated incident. The key is that the actions or comments are viewed as demeaning and unacceptable to the recipient. (NUJ 2008: 24)

Dignity is thus threatened by demeaning comments (or other actions) that refer to personal characteristics of the offended individual. This effort fits well into the Kantian Formula of Humanity, interpreted as a requirement not to humiliate other people.

A member of the European parliament claimed that a common European solution for refugees was 'first of all a matter of humanity and of human dignity' (McAllister 2015). Again, this example would fit well with the Kantian formula of humanity, this time interpreted as a requirement to respect other people's reasonable sense of purpose and their sense of self-worth. Taking Syrian refugees as an example, one could argue the following. Given that neither their reasonable sense of purpose nor their sense of self-worth is respected by the civil war situation and the dictatorship in their native Syria, respecting their dignity requires first of all offering them a safe place and a possibility to establish livelihoods [Whether human beings, in this case Europeans, have a global duty to respect the Kantian dignity of distant strangers is a question that cannot be resolved here. John Rawls might reply with 'no' (Rawls 1999b) and Thomas Pogge emphatically with 'yes' (Pogge 2001)].

We have given examples from the world of sport: the rapid exit of all northern hemisphere teams from the 2015 Rugby World Cup and Zinedine Zidane's famous headbutt in the 2006 FIFA World Cup. The former could easily be linked to dignity, in the sense of rank and position: that is northern hemisphere teams lost their ranking in rugby. The headbutt was interpreted in two different ways: a German journalist was appalled and claimed Zidane had lost all dignity, while a French journalist claimed he had been defending his dignity (assuming the headbutt was in response to an insult to Zidane's family). On both counts, comportment dignity would have been at stake, with a hint of virtue dignity. From the perspective of the German journalist, one would assume, offences against etiquette, good manners, restraint and willpower were involved in the act. The French journalist, one could surmise, would talk about courage, honour, pride etc., when describing the attack as some kind of self-defence against humiliation.

Nelson Mandela and former Norwegian Minister of International Development Hilde F. Johnson noted that extreme poverty violates human dignity. Given the impact extreme poverty has on human lives, the dignity claim fits into both variants of intrinsic dignity. Extreme poverty is a violation both of the sanctity of life and of the individual's sense of purpose and sense of self-worth.

In *Les Miserables*, Victor Hugo evocatively describes the pain and suffering of extreme poverty, also using the term dignity. He writes:

> A terrible thing it is, containing days without bread, nights without sleep, evenings without a candle, a hearth without a fire, weeks without work, a future without a hope, a coat out at the elbows, an old hat which evokes the laughter of young girls, a door which one finds locked on one at night because one's rent is not paid, … the sneers of neighbours, humiliations, dignity trampled on, work of whatever nature accepted, disgusts, bitterness, despondency. (Hugo 1887)

Before commenting on Hugo's description, another quotation is offered. In one of the most famous books in English literature, *Wuthering Heights*, a child of unknown parentage, Heathcliff, falls in love with Cathy, with whom he played during his childhood on the Yorkshire moors. One of the reasons he cannot marry Cathy, even though their passion is mutual, is that he is poor and of unknown parentage. One day Nelly Dean, the servant who narrates the bulk of the story, says to Heathcliff:

> Who knows, but your father was Emperor of China, and your mother an Indian queen, each of them able to buy up, with one week's income, Wuthering Heights and Thrushcross Grange together? And you were kidnapped by wicked sailors and brought to England. Were I in your place, I would frame high notions of my birth; and the thought of what I was should give me courage and dignity. … (Brontë 1996: 41)

Nelly clearly empathises with Heathcliff's solitude and lack of roots. She tells him that his dignity—his sense of self-worth and pride—can come from his imagination. A sense of self-worth is important for two of the five concepts of dignity. It is a virtue, but at the same time respect for other people's sense of self-worth is an essential part of Kantian dignity (Fig. 2.12).

It is this sense of self-worth that is undermined in Victor Hugo's description of serious poverty, through 'the sneers of neighbours', 'the laughter of young girls'

Fig. 2.12 Sense of self-worth and dignity

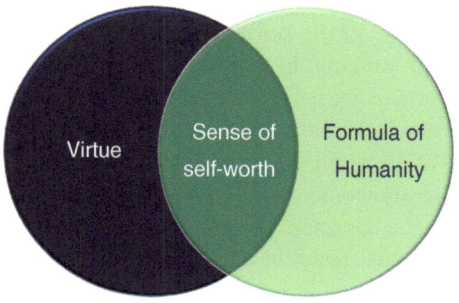

and the 'humiliations' leading to bitterness and despondency, 'dignity trampled on'. Likewise, attacks on Heathcliff's sense of self-worth are related to his poverty and inability to do in life what he wishes to do, to fulfil his life plans, including to marry Cathy. As such a link can be found between dignity as a virtue and dignity as in the Formula of Humanity through the sense of self-worth that is important in both.

David Grossman describes a 'dignified world' as a world 'where every human found the one meant for them, where every love was true love and where one lived eternally' (Grossman 2003: 250, DS translation). This is a clear ascription of dignity to a precise state of affairs. He could also have called this world a 'golden world', 'an ideal world', a 'utopian world', a 'dream world' or any other positive term. It is unclear why Grossman calls this world dignified, and the quote cannot be fitted into the taxonomy, nor can it be called vague. However, one could argue that it is not important to fit a completely unrealistic vision into the general understanding of a concept, which is meant to be of some use in ethical and other debates.

In 2015, the Singapore President's Challenge Social Enterprise of the Year award was given to Project Dignity, which gives 'employment, training and dignity to people with disabilities' (Straits Times 2015). The project has several sub-activities, one of them being Dignity Mama, which sells donated used books in hospitals. This charity's work too can be linked neatly with Kantian dignity. To be able to contribute to society through trained employment may be more difficult for disabled citizens than for non-disabled citizens. To assist in this enterprise could be interpreted as giving disabled citizens better means to develop further their sense of purpose and self-worth.

In August 2015, Gill Pharaoh died at an assisted suicide clinic in Switzerland at the age of 75. She was a retired palliative care nurse, 'a contented, affluent woman, in good health, with a loving partner, two children and a grandson' (Douglas Home 2015). 'I do not want people to remember me as a sort of old lady hobbling up the road with a trolley' (Donnelly 2015). For the Spectator, Isabel Hardman wrote that 'not everyone will think that being "an old lady hobbling up the road with a trolley" is an unbearable loss of dignity, as Pharaoh did' (Hardman 2015). Pharaoh's concerns fall into the area of comportment dignity. A UK study showed that 'dignity was salient to the concerns of older people' (Woolhead et al. 2004: 166) and that it consisted of elements such as respectable appearance. 'Participants stated that lack of attention to people's appearance by hospital or residential staff, such as haphazard buttoning of clothes or dishevelled dress, reduced dignity' (Woolhead et al. 2004: 166).

To sum up: when we searched for examples of dignity being used as a concept, we encountered a range of examples that did not fit into the given taxonomy. However, none was precise enough to refine or broaden the existing taxonomy. Instead, they were all as vague as Ruth Macklin and others have claimed. They used dignity as a slogan rather than with a precise meaning. These will be discussed briefly now.

2.5.1 Dignity and Vagueness

Friedrich Schiller's 'Die Künstler' (The Artists) is a beautiful poem about dignity, but what it means is not clear.

Der Menschheit Würde	*The dignity of Man,*
ist in eure Hand gegeben,	*into your hands is given*
Bewahret sie!	*Protector be!*
Sie sinkt mit euch!	*It sinks with you!*
Mit euch wird sie sich heben!	*With you it is arisen!* (Schiller n.d.)

Schiller could be referring to almost all concepts of dignity. He could be appealing to people to be virtuous, to behave with propriety, to adhere to the Formula of Humanity or to respect the sanctity of a life. As a result, one can conclude that his use of dignity is vague (which is less of an offence for a poem than a political manifesto, of course).

In 2015, Pope Francis addressed the US Congress as follows:

> Your own responsibility as members of Congress is to enable this country, by your legislative activity, to grow as a nation. ... You are called to defend and preserve the dignity of your fellow citizens in the tireless and demanding pursuit of the common good, for this is the chief aim of all politics. (Francis 2015)

While Pope Francis spoke out against the death penalty as an affront to dignity at the same event, this excerpt from his speech is vague and slogan-like. To preserve the dignity of citizens, as the chief aim of all politics, can mean almost anything or nothing. It can refer to the safety of citizens, their welfare, their prospects and more. To subsume this all under one heading, dignity, is unhelpful when trying to understand what is being advocated.

Maithripala Sirisena took office as President of Sri Lanka in 2015. He noted at a Commonwealth Heads of Government Meeting attended by the Queen in November that year that he was satisfied with progress made on behalf of his people. He emphasised improvements in the areas of 'poverty eradication, promotion of trade, sustainable development, involvement of youth in development activities, growth, equality and dignity of the citizens' (CHOGM 2015).

> The President said that what is important is common values and not the power of wealth. He emphasized the imperative need to achieve growth, equality and dignity for the people. (CHOGM 2015)

The President listed areas his government's policies were focusing on to improve the life of Sri Lankan citizens. However, it was unclear which improvements were related to the dignity of citizens. Hence, one could say that this, like Pope Francis's exhortation to the US Congress, was an instance of the vague use of the concept, as it not only does not fit into the current taxonomy, but fails to suggest any additional element to the taxonomy.

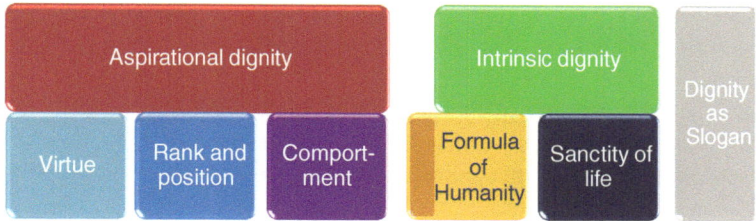

Fig. 2.13 Six types of dignity

In 2010, Tsutomu Yamaguchi died. He had survived both the Hiroshima and the Nagasaki atom bombs. He was described as 'both the luckiest man in the world and the unluckiest' (The Week Staff 2010) and quoted as saying the following:

> The reason that I hate the atomic bomb is because of what it does to the dignity of human beings (Ryall 2010).

While the obvious death-bringing power of atom bombs could link this statement to the Catholic understanding of the sanctity of life, Yamaguchi's claim, however moving, is too vague to verify. A separate category of dignity as slogan will therefore be added to the taxonomy. 'Slogan', in this context, stands for a memorable phrase that is suitable for repetition and will create different ideas in different listeners without requiring precision (Fig. 2.13).

One response to the 'dignity as slogan' category came from Ruth Macklin, who requested that the concept be replaced by respect for persons.

2.5.2 *Could Dignity Be Replaced with Respect for Persons?*

In 2003, Ruth Macklin famously argued that dignity 'is a useless concept in medical ethics and can be eliminated without any loss of content'. One should simply talk about respect for persons and their autonomy (Macklin 2003: 586). Harvard professor Steven Pinker went even further and argued in response to a 555-page report on dignity from the US President's Council on Bioethics (Pellegrino et al. 2008) that it is 'a squishy, subjective notion' used mostly 'to condemn anything that gives someone the creeps' (Pinker 2008).

Macklin's article was an editorial just over one page long, which received a remarkable 35 official responses in the BMJ (British Medical Journal). By comparison, Amartya Sen's landmark article 'Missing Women' in the BMJ (Sen 1992) received none, and his editorial 'Missing Women—Revisited' (Sen 2003) received 15. Macklin's argument can be summarised as follows:

1. An analysis of appeals to dignity reveals that they are either very vague or used to describe something that could be captured more precisely with other concepts.
2. When the term is used in the context of health care and medical research, 'dignity' means nothing other than 'respect of persons', which requires informed consent, the protection of confidentiality and the avoidance of discrimination and abusive practices.
3. When the term is used in the context of human cloning, the concept is so hopelessly vague that it is impossible to determine criteria for when it is violated or not. As a result, it is a mere slogan.
4. The reason why dignity is used in so many debates in health care ethics is the use of religious sources.
5. Macklin concludes: 'Although the aetiology may remain a mystery, the diagnosis is clear. Dignity is a useless concept in medical ethics and can be eliminated without any loss of content' (Macklin 2003: 1420).

As early as 1840, similar concerns were raised by Arthur Schopenhauer (1788–1860) when commenting on Immanuel Kant's use of the term 'dignity' to mean absolute inner worth. Schopenhauer predicted that dignity would develop into the shibboleth[20] of all thoughtless philosophers: a hollow hyperbole inhabited by a nagging worm, the *contradictio in adjecto*.[21] This means that absolute inner worth carries a contradiction in itself, like 'square circle'. According to Schopenhauer, 'worth' is the estimation of one thing in comparison to another, invariably involving relativity, as the Stoics and Romans already recognised:

> [W]orth is the remuneration or equivalent value for something fixed by an expert; just as it is said that wheat is exchanged for barley plus a mule (Dioegenes Laertius, cited in Schopenhauer 2009: 166).

Kant's understanding of dignity—an incomparable, unconditional, absolute worth—is, like many things in philosophy, according to Schopenhauer, a word for an idea that cannot be thought, such as the highest number or the largest space.

How can one respond to Schopenhauer and Macklin? While Schopenhauer objected to dignity in its totality, without even suggesting a replacement concept, he objected mainly to Kant's definition of dignity as absolute inner worth. If one links Kantian dignity to the second formula of the categorical imperative, as in our earlier section on Kant, the *contradictio in adjecto* disappears.

---

[20]A shibboleth is a peculiarity (originally relating to pronunciation) that reveals to which group one belongs. It goes back to the Old Testament: '[W]hen any fugitive from Ephraim asked them, "Let me cross over," the men from Gilead would ask him, "Are you an Ephraimite?" If he said "No," they would order him, "Pronounce the word 'Shibboleth' right now." If he said "Sibboleth," not being able to pronounce it correctly, they would seize him and slaughter him there at the fords of the Jordan River. During those days 42,000 descendants of Ephraim died that way' (Judges 12:5–6, International Standard Version).

[21]Similar to oxymoron, a *contradictio in adjecto* implies that an adjective added to a noun has caused a contradiction, e.g. 'married bachelor', 'living corpse'.

As for Ruth Macklin's suggestion, one might surmise that Macklin encountered the use of dignity as slogan frequently. This would probably be highly frustrating when one is dealing with pressing practical problems in medical ethics. It is unlikely that her short editorial was meant to criticise the widespread use of the word 'dignity' in legal instruments and other areas such as fiction. That being so, Suzy Killmister responded to Macklin's assertion in an article in the BMJ's Journal of Medical Ethics entitled 'Dignity: Not Such a Useless Concept':

> In her 2003 article in the British Medical Journal, Ruth Macklin provocatively declared dignity to be a useless concept. ... A recent response to Macklin has challenged this claim. Doris Schroeder attempts to rescue dignity by positing ... [several] distinct concepts that fall under the one umbrella term. She argues that much of the confusion surrounding dignity is due to the lack of disambiguation among these ... [different] concepts (Killmister 2010: 160).

In conclusion, Killmister claims that 'Macklin's assessment of dignity as a useless concept was premature', as a disambiguated concept of dignity 'can continue to serve as a guiding principle in medical ethics' (Killmister 2010: 164). In terms of the disambiguation developed further in this book, Macklin's criticism applies only to intrinsic dignity as defined by Kant, as well as dignity as slogan, a focus too narrow to do the concept justice.

2.6   A Common Core of Dignity Building Blocks?

'Such high hopes, and to end like this.'

'Yes, I agree, it is humiliating. But perhaps that is a good point to start from again. Perhaps that is what I must learn to accept. To start at ground level. With nothing. Not with nothing but. With nothing. No cards, no weapons, no property, no rights, no dignity.'

'Like a dog.'

'Yes, like a dog.'

Coetzee (1999: 205)

Before we conclude this discussion of dignity in the West and move on to dignity in the Middle East, are there any building blocks of dignity that are common across the five elements (setting aside dignity as slogan), namely: dignity as virtue, dignity as rank and position, dignity as comportment, dignity equated with Kant's Formula of Humanity and dignity as sanctity of life? Do they have a common core? We would argue that self-worth may be such a common denominator (Fig. 2.14).

In the philosophical and psychology literature, self-esteem and self-respect are described in detail. For John Rawls, 'the most important primary good is that of self-respect '(Rawls 1999a: 386). Rawls uses 'self-respect' and 'self-esteem' interchangeably.

> We may define self-respect (or self-esteem) as having two aspects. First of all ... it includes a person's sense of his own value, his secure conviction that his conception of his good, his

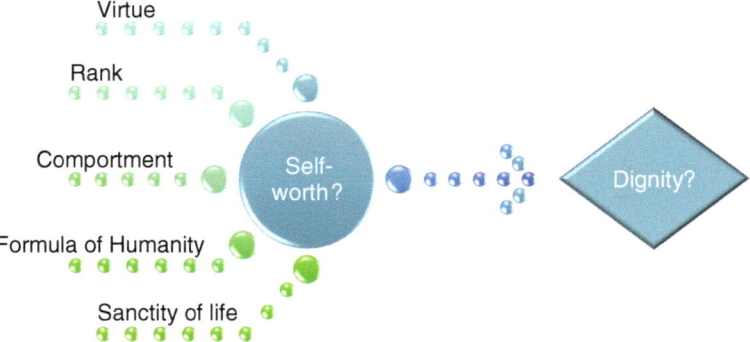

Fig. 2.14 Self-worth and dignity

plan of life, is worth carrying out. And second, self-respect implies a confidence in one's ability, so far as it is within one's power, to fulfil one's intentions. When we feel that our plans are of little value, we cannot pursue them with pleasure or take delight in their execution. Nor plagued by failure and self-doubt can we continue in our endeavours. It is clear then why self-respect is a primary good. Without it nothing may seem worth doing. … All desire and activity becomes empty and vain, and we sink into apathy and cynicism. (Rawls 1999a: 386)

Feminist writers in particular, have criticised the equation of self-respect with self-esteem. For instance, Michele Moody-Adams argues that self-esteem is confidence in one's life plan and that self-respect is having a solid sense of one's own worth (Moody-Adams 1995). By this definition, it is clear why they would differ. Persons in captivity would have no reasonable confidence in their life plans, but could still maintain a solid sense of their own worth. This also aligns with Laurence Thomas's definition of self-respect: 'A person has self-respect … if he has the conviction that he is deserving of full moral status, and so the basic rights of that status' (Thomas 1995).

The term 'self-worth' has been chosen here for two reasons: first, to create a link with the Kantian understanding of absolute inner worth, given that Kant was one of the most influential Western theorists of dignity; and second, to avoid disputes about the distinctions between self-respect and self-esteem. It is possible, for instance, to undermine self-respect (understood as a solid sense of one's own worth as a being who deserves respect and has life plans) through the constant undermining of self-esteem (the ability to believe in one's capacity to realise one's life plans). For example, parents who constantly criticise their children as not being good enough, not being able to perform to their parents' expectations, who never give praise, may very well have this effect. Choosing the term 'self-worth' as encompassing both self-respect and self-esteem avoids having to specify the undefinable borderline between the two.

Can virtue, rank, comportment, Kant's Formula of Humanity and sanctity of life all be linked to self-worth in the context of dignity? (Table 2.3)

Table 2.3 Can self-worth be linked to all Western concepts of dignity?

Virtue	A sense of self-worth is highly prominent in virtue ethics. For instance, Aristotelian *eudaimonia* (happiness) comes to those who always behave virtuously and live life as it ought to be lived. This way of life links well to a sense of self-worth and pride in virtue
Rank	Rank and a sense of self-worth are only indirectly linked. Generally, if the outside world reacts with approval to a person (as many are likely to if the person is highly ranked) this could be one contributing factor—psychologically speaking—for a stronger sense of self-worth
Comportment	Dignified comportment is usually associated with expressing a sense of self-worth, for instance in posture and general demeanour
Formula of Humanity	For Kant, a sense of self-worth is a duty to oneself, and therefore an essential element of human dignity
Sanctity of life	There is no obvious link between the Catholic sanctity of life and a person's sense of self-worth

As has already been noted, a strong sense of self-worth is the overlapping consensus between virtue theory's approach to dignity and the Kantian understanding of dignity. This is pleasing in so far as these are the two main philosophical theories that were examined. Catholicism is a religion and not a philosophical theory, and dignity as rank and dignity as comportment are only minor interpretations of the concept. One could therefore argue that, from a Western perspective, respecting and protecting human beings' sense of self-worth could be a step towards overcoming the differences between aspirational and intrinsic dignity.

2.7   Concluding on the Dignity Riddles

At the outset of the discussion on dignity from a Western perspective, two riddles were set.

Riddle 1:   The German constitution states in article 1(1) that 'human dignity is inviolable' *and* that 'its protection is the duty of all state powers' (Germany 1949: art. 1 I, DS translation). Why would something that is *inviolable* (meaning secure from attack, assault or trespass) need protection?

Riddle 2:   Who is right? According to Germany's most famous poet, Johann Wolfgang von Goethe (1749–1832), 'a laurel is much easier bound than a dignified head for it found'. In other words, dignity crowns only a few select heads. But according to Germany's most famous philosopher, Immanuel Kant (1724–1804), dignity is intrinsic and cannot be denied even to a vicious man. In other words, dignity is not selective; in Kant's interpretation, it belongs to all [rational] human beings

To come to a conclusion on the first dignity riddle, one has to ask: which concept of dignity does the German constitution support? And why does the constitution allow a logical difficulty in its first two statements?

There are two possible answers. Given that the German constitution appeals to intrinsic dignity, it could refer to the Kantian or the Catholic interpretation. Let us start with the first possibility: the German constitution uses the Kantian interpretation of dignity, the Formula of Humanity. Human beings possess a dignity by which they command respect for themselves from all other rational beings. This dignity gives them the right always to exact respect for their reasonable sense of purpose and self-worth. Human beings must never be instrumentalised for the sole use of others without their reasonable consent.

It was observed earlier that, grammatically speaking, the German constitution's first two statements, namely that human dignity *is inviolable* and that all state powers *must protect it* are contradictory. Why would something that is inviolable need protection? Dignity is either violable and needs protection or it is inviolable and does not need protection. This riddle can only be resolved by reference to German history, German jurisprudence and a comparison with other constitutions. As noted, the Iranian and the Saudi Arabian constitutions do not regard dignity as inviolable. In the Iranian constitution, dignity can be overridden in cases sanctioned by law. The Saudi Arabian constitution links dignity only with privacy rights and prohibits dignity violations by the media.

Examples of dignity violations are coercion and torture, as in the Daschner case (see Box 2.1). Other examples given by German legal experts are slavery and human trafficking, forms of discrimination which deny that certain persons belong to humanity, overriding the will through the use of truth serum, hypnosis or systematic humiliation, and intrusions and medical manipulation for reproductive purposes (Bourcarde 2004: 40) (Fig. 2.15). It is here that the Kantian interpretation of dignity makes more sense for the German constitution than the Catholic understanding of the sanctity of human life. First, none of the above instances of dignity violations has as its main purpose to threaten human life. Something else is at stake in systematic humiliation, slavery or torture, namely the instrumentalisation

Fig. 2.15 Possible dignity violations

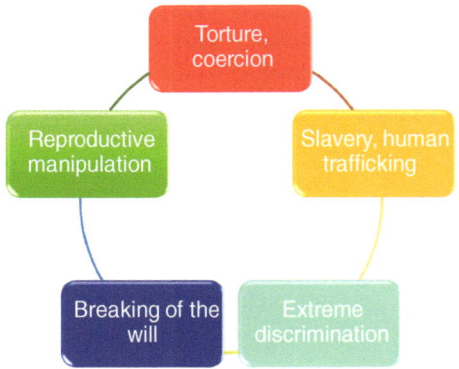

of some for the sole use of others. Second, only rational beings (in the widest sense, for instance beings who are not in a persistent vegetative state) can have their will overridden by truth sera or can be systematically humiliated.

What the German constitution aims to secure with its first statement that human dignity is inviolable is a *complete* ban by the state on dignity violations such as the ones listed. Naming this principle as the first principle of the constitution is an attempt to prevent for all time the return of the atrocities committed by the German state in the 1930s and 1940s. According to jurisprudence specialists, it means that—in extreme cases—the state is allowed to intervene in all other basic rights (including the sanctity of life), but never in the principle of dignity (Bourcarde 2004: 39). Even if, as in the Daschner case, the deputy police chief assumes that a child victim of abduction may be dying of thirst in a hideout while the lone abductor is in police custody, the German constitution cannot even sanction the threat of coercion (as happened in this case, in contravention of the law). In this sense, human dignity is inviolable in the German constitution: dignity violations are always illegal and offend the first principle of the German constitution understood in a Kantian sense.

However, even if state forces always obeyed this rule (and the Daschner case shows that they do not), dignity violations (e.g. human trafficking) would still occur, which is why the second German constitutional principle states that the protection of human dignity is the duty of all state powers. Hence, to answer the first dignity riddle: the German constitution expresses a belief in Kantian dignity that is so strong that it produces a contradiction in its first two principles. This can be attributed to the powerful obligation felt by the fathers and mothers of the constitution to avoid, for all time, utterly unjustifiable violations of the reasonable sense of purpose and self-worth of any human being.

This tenet is so strong that it also deviates from Kant's belief that the Formula of Humanity applies not to all human beings, but only to those with rational faculties. The constitutional prohibition against dignity violations applies to all human beings. It is here that the dignity understanding of the German constitution aligns most closely with the Catholic precept of the sanctity of life.

Turning to the second dignity riddle, who is right, Goethe or Kant? Is dignity a crown that decorates only a few heads or an intrinsic property of all human beings? The answer to this riddle was given with the taxonomy of dignity. For some interpretations of dignity, Goethe is right, for some Kant. Dignity as virtue, as rank and as dignified comportment are selective. Dignity as understood by Kant (with the small proviso regarding the realm of dignity being aligned with the realm of rationality) and dignity as understood by the Catholic Church are intrinsic. Hence, Goethe is right and Kant is right, each for a different understanding of dignity.

We have therefore been able to resolve both dignity riddles, and also clarified the term through systematic disambiguation. The next section examines what dignity means in the Koran, written from a spiritual, rather than disambiguating, analytical perspective.

References

Aranda K, Jones A (2010) Dignity in health-care: a critical exploration using feminism and theories of recognition. Nursing Inquiry 17(3):248–256

Aristotle (2000) Nicomachean Ethics. Translated by R Crisp. Cambridge University Press, Cambridge

Auster P (2004) Oracle night. Faber and Faber, New York

Bentham J (1831) An introduction to the principles of morals and legislation. Kindle version

Brecht B (2003) Poetry and Prose. Bloomsbury, The German Library, London

Beyleveld D, Brownsword R (2001) Human dignity in bioethics and biolaw. Oxford University Press, Oxford

Birnbacher D (1995) Mehrdeutigkeiten im Begriff der Menschenwuerde. Forschungsgruppe Weltanschauungen in Deutschland, Textarchiv TA-1995-8, http://docplayer.org/21535997-Mehrdeutigkeiten-im-begriff-der-menschenwuerde.html

Bishops of Texas and the Texas Conference of Catholic Health Facilities (2006) An Interim pastoral statement on artificial nutrition and hydration. In: Caplan AL, McCartney JJ, Sisti DA (eds) The case of Terri Schiavo: ethics at the end of life. Prometheus Books, New York, p 189–194

Bontekoe R (2008) The nature of dignity. Lexington Books, Lanham MD

Bourcarde K (2004) Folter im Rechtsstaat? Die Bundesrepublik nach dem Entführungsfall Jakob von Metzler. Self-published, Gießen, Germany. http://www.bourcarde.eu/texte/folter_im_rechtsstaat.pdf

Brecher B (2007) Torture and the ticking bomb. Wiley-Blackwell, Oxford

Brontë E (1996) Wuthering Heights. Dover Publications, Mineola NY

Callahan D (1995) Bioethics. In: Post SG (ed) Encyclopedia of bioethics, vol 1, 3rd edn. Macmillan Reference, New York, p 278–286

Child LM (1854) Memoirs of Madame de Staël and of Madame Roland. CS Francis, New York and Boston. https://ia801409.us.archive.org/5/items/memoirsmadamede00chilgoog/memoirsmadamede00chilgoog.pdf

CHOGM: President emphasizes need to ensure people's dignity (2015) Daily Mirror (Sri Lanka), 27 November. http://www.dailymirror.lk/97141/eed-to-ensure-people-s-dignity

Cicero MT (1913) De officiis. Translated by W Miller. Loeb Edition. Harvard University Press, Cambridge MA. http://www.stoics.com/cicero_book.html

Coe J (1997) The house of sleep. Penguin Viking Books, London

Coetzee JM (1999) Disgrace. Vintage, London

Cohen C (2001) The animal rights debate. Rowman and Littlefield, New York

Crwys-Williams J (1997) In the words of Nelson Mandela. Penguin Books, London

Dan-Cohen M (2015) Introduction: dignity and its (dis)content. In: Waldron J (ed) Dignity, rank, and rights. Oxford University Press, Oxford, p 3–10

Dart T (2006) Zidane is still a hero to philosophers and fans. The Times, 13 July. http://www.thetimes.co.uk/tto/sport/football/article2280263.ece

De Chirico L (2005) The dignity of the human person: towards an evangelical reading of the theology of personhood of Vatican II. Evangelical Quarterly 77(3):249–259

Denenberg B (1995) Nelson Mandela: No easy walk to freedom. Scholastic, New York

Der Mordfall Jakob von Metzler: Ein Verbrechen und seine Folgen (The Jakob von Metzler murder case: A crime and its consequenes) (2006) Zweites Deutsches Fernsehen (ZDF), 26 July, 22:45

Dillon RS (2014) Respect. In Zalta EN (ed) The Stanford encyclopedia of philosophy (Winter 2016 edition). The Metaphysics Research Lab, Center for the Study of Language and In-formation, Stanford University, Stanford, CA. https://plato.stanford.edu/entries/respect/

Donnelly L (2015) Healthy retired nurse ends her life because old age 'is awful'. The Tele-graph, 2 August. http://www.telegraph.co.uk/news/health/11778859/Healthy-retired-nurse-ends-her-life-because-old-age-is-awful.html

Dostoevsky F (1917) Crime and punishment. Translated by C Garnett. PF Collier & Son, New York. http://www.bartleby.com/318/32.html

Douglas Home C (2015) Best to travel hopefully until all hope has been removed. The Herald (Scotland), 4 August. http://www.heraldscotland.com/news/13527139.Colette_Douglas_Home__Best_to_travel_hopefully_until_all_hope_has_been_removed/

Dworkin R, Nagel T, Nozick R, Rawls J, Scanlon T, Thomson JJ (1997) Assisted suicide: the philosophers' brief. The New York Review of Books, 27 March. http://www.nybooks.com/articles/1997/03/27/assisted-suicide-the-philosophers-brief/

Dylan B (1991) Dignity. Special Rider Music. http://bobdylan.com/songs/dignity/

Eibach U (2008) Protection of life and human dignity: the German debate between Christian norms and secular expectations. Christian Bioethics 14(1):58–77

EU (2008) Consolidated versions of the Treaty on European Union and the Treaty on the functioning of the European Union. Council of the European Union, Brussels. http://eur-lex.europa.eu/legal-content/EN/TXT/HTML/?uri=CELEX:12012M/TXT&from=en

Fadiman C (1955) War and peace. In: Party of one: the selected writings of Clifton Fadiman. The World Publishing Company, Cleveland NY, p 176–202. https://archive.org/details/partyofone030253mbp

Foot P (1978) Virtues and vices. In: Virtues and vices and other essays in moral philosophy. Blackwell, Oxford, p 1–18

Francis (2015) Transcript: Pope Francis's speech to Congress. The Washington Post, 24 Sep-tember. https://www.washingtonpost.com/local/social-issues/transcript-pope-franciss-speech-to-congress/2015/09/24/6d7d7ac8-62bf-11e5-8e9e-dce8a2a2a679_story.html?utm_term=.cd7ab00a7723

Gandhi MK (1920) The doctrine of the sword. Young India, 11 August https://www.gandhiheritageportal.org/datalink/files/ghp_journals/journal_image_3/young_india_vol2_img251.jpg

Germany (1949) Grundgesetz für die Bundesrepublik Deutschland. http://www.bundestag.de/bundestag/aufgaben/rechtsgrundlagen/grundgesetz

Goethe JW von (n.d.) Sämtliche Werke. Insel Verlag, Leipzig

Green RM (2001) What does it mean to use someone as 'a means only': rereading Kant. Ken-nedy Institute of Ethics Journal 11(3):247–261

Grossman D (2003) Sei du mir das Messer. Fischer Taschenbuch, Frankfurt

Hardman I (2015) Assisted dying will make old age seem unbearable. The Spectator, 3 August. http://blogs.spectator.co.uk/2015/08/assisted-dying-will-make-old-age-seem-unbearable/

Hayry M (2005) The tension between self governance and absolute inner worth in Kant's moral philosophy. Journal of Medical Ethics 31:645–647

Hill TE Jr (1991) Autonomy and self-respect. Cambridge University Press, Cambridge

Hill TE Jr (1992) Dignity and practical reason in Kant's moral theory. Cornell University Press, 'Ithaca NY

Hofmann B (2002) Respect for patient dignity in primary health care: the critical appraisal. Scandinavian Journal of Primary Health Care 20:88–91

Hörzu (2015) Mit Moral und Würde. TV programme description of 'Die Frau, die sich traut'. 9 October. ARTE. http://www.arte.tv/guide/de/047059-000-A/die-frau-die-sich-traut

Hospital JT (1990) History is false but this is true. The New York Times, 25 March. http://www.nytimes.com/1990/03/25/books/history-is-false-but-this-is-true.html

Hugo V (1887) Les misérables. Translated by IF Hopgood. Thomas Y Cromwell & Co, New York

India (2015) The Constitution of India. Government of India, Ministry of Law and Justice (Legislative Department), New Delhi. http://lawmin.nic.in/olwing/coi/coi-english/coi-4March2016.pdf

Iran (1979) Constitution of the Islamic Republic of Iran. Government of the Islamic Republic of Iran. http://www.iranonline.com/iran/iran-info/government/constitution.html

Jenkins P (2004) Police trial divides Germany over state-sanctioned violence. Financial Times, 19 November, p. 4

John Paul II (1995) Evangelium vitae (The gospel of life). Librera Editrice Vaticana. http://w2.
    vatican.va/content/john-paul-ii/en/encyclicals/documents/hf_jp-ii_enc_25031995_evangelium-
    vitae.html
John Paul II (2004) Address of John Paul II to the participants in the international congress on
    'Life-sustaining treatments and vegetative state: scientific advances and ethical dilemmas'.
    Librera Editrice Vaticana. https://w2.vatican.va/content/john-paul-ii/en/speeches/2004/march/
    documents/hf_jp-ii_spe_20040320_congress-fiamc.html
Johnson HF (2005) Poverty and global justice: Some challenges ahead. In: Pogge T, Follesdal A
    (eds) Real world justice. Springer, Berlin, p 21–26
Kant I (1990) Metaphysische Anfangsgründe der Tugendlehre. Felix Meiner Verlag, Hamburg
Kant I (1996) The metaphysics of morals. Translated by M Gregor. Cambridge University Press,
    Cambridge.
Kant I (1997) Groundwork of the metaphysics of morals. Translated by M Gregor. Cambridge
    University Press, Cambridge
Kant I (1998) Critique of pure reason. Translated by AW Wood. Cambridge University Press,
    Cambridge
Kateb G (2011) Human dignity. Harvard University Press, Cambridge MA
Killmister S (2010) Dignity: not such a useless concept. Journal of Medical Ethics 36(3):160–164
Korsgaard CM (1998) Introduction to the groundwork of the metaphysics of morals. In: Gregor M
    (ed) Groundwork of the metaphysics of morals. Cambridge University Press, Cambridge,
    p vii–xxx
Lebech M (2004) What is human dignity? In: Lebech M (ed) Maynooth philosophical papers:
    Issue 2. Faculty of Philosophy, National University of Ireland Maynooth, Ireland, p 59–69
Lee P (2001). Personhood, dignity, suicide and euthanasia. National Catholic Bioethics Quarterly
    1(3):329–344
Löer C (2006) Der Verlust der Würde. Kölner Stadt-Anzeiger, 10 July. http://www.ksta.de/der-
    verlust-der-wuerde-13541050
Luban D (2005) Lawyers as upholders of human dignity (when they aren't busy assaulting it).
    University of Illinois Law Review: 815–845. http://scholarship.law.georgetown.edu/facpub/
    147/
Machiavelli N (2015) The prince. Translated by WK Marriott. Wisehouse Classics, Sweden
Macklin R (2003) Dignity is a useless concept. BMJ 327:1419–1420
Mandela N (2004) Mandela's wish for South Africa. SouthAfrica.info. http://www.southafrica.
    info/mandela/mandela-10yearsaddress.htm
Márai S (2005) Die Nacht vor der Scheidung (original Hungarian title: Válás Budán). Piper
    Verlag, Munich
Margalit A (1998) The decent society. Harvard University Press, Cambridge MA
Markwell H (2005) End-of-life: a Catholic view. Lancet 366:1132–1135
McAllister D (2015) Europe's refugee crisis requires a European response. The Telegraph, 15
    September. http://www.telegraph.co.uk/news/worldnews/europe/11866790/Europes-refugee-
    crisis-requires-a-European-response.html
McHugh JT (2001) Building a culture of life: a Catholic perspective. Christian Bioethics 7(3)
    441–452
Moody-Adams M (1995) Race, class, and the social construction of self-respect. In: Dillon RS
    (ed) Dignity, character and self-respect. Routledge, New York, p 271–289
Murdoch I (1980) Nuns and soldiers. Chatto & Windus, London
Neumann M (2000) Did Kant respect persons? Res Publica 6:285–299
NUJ (2008) Stop bullying: challenging bullies and achieving dignity at work. National Union of
    Journalists, London. https://www.nuj.org.uk/documents/stop-bullying-nuj-handbook/
Nussbaum MC (2000) Women and human development: the capabilities approach. Cambridge
    University Press, Cambridge
Paton HJ (1948) The moral law. Hutchinson University Library, London

Pellegrino ED, Schulman A, Merrill TW (2008) Human dignity and bioethics: essays commissioned by the President's Council on Bioethics. The President's Council on Bioethics, Washington DC. https://repository.library.georgetown.edu/handle/10822/559351

Pico della Mirandola G (2012) Oration on the dignity of man (Oratio de hominis dignitate). Edited by F Borghesi, M Papio, M Riva. Cambridge University Press NY

Pinker S (2008) The stupidity of dignity. The New Republic, 28 May. https://newrepublic.com/article/64674/the-stupidity-dignity

Pogge T (ed) (2001) Global justice. Blackwell Publishers, Oxford

R. v Kapp [2008] SCC [Supreme Court of Canada] 41

Rawls J (1999a) A theory of justice (rev edn). Oxford University Press, Oxford

Rawls J (1999b) The law of peoples. Harvard University Press, Cambridge MA

Reason M (2015) Mark Reason: Northern hemisphere rugby has lost its dignity. Rugby Heaven, 21 October. http://www.stuff.co.nz/sport/rugby/opinion/73200720/Mark-Reason-Northern-hemisphere-rugby-has-lost-its-dignity

Ricoeur P (1995) Oneself as another. University of Chicago Press, Chicago

Rigali JF, Lori WE (2008) Human dignity and the end of life. America: The National Catholic Review 199(3)13–15. http://www.americamagazine.org/sites/default/files/issues/cf/pdfs/663_1.pdf

Roberts J (1988) German philosophy: An introduction, Polity Press, Oxford

Rosen M (2012) Dignity: Its history and meaning. Harvard University Press, Cambridge MA

Ross WD (1969) Kant's ethical theory. a commentary on the Grundlegung zur Metaphysik der Sitten. Clarendon Press, Oxford

Rückert S (2004) Straflos schuldig. Die Zeit 59(53):1

Russia (1993) Constitution of the Russian Federation. Government of the Russian Federation. http://www.departments.bucknell.edu/russian/const/ch1.html

Ryall J (2010) Japanese man who survived two atomic bombs dies. The Telegraph, 6 January. http://www.telegraph.co.uk/news/worldnews/asia/japan/6939379/Japanese-man-who-survived-two-atomic-bombs-dies.html

Sartre J-P (1958) Being and nothingness. Translated by HE Barnes. Methuen & Co, London

Saudi Arabia (1992) Saudi Arabia: Constitution. Government of the Kingdom of Saudi Arabia. https://www.unodc.org/tldb/pdf/Saudi_Arabia_const_1992.doc

Schaber P (2012) Menschenwürde. Reclam, Stuttgart

Schiller F (n.d.) Die Künstler (The artists). Translated by M Wertz. Schiller Institute. http://www.schillerinstitute.org/transl/trans_schil_1poems.html#the_artist

Schopenhauer A (2009) The two fundamental problems of ethics. Translated by C Janaway. Cambridge University Press, Cambridge

Schreiner O (1989) The story of an African farm. Virago Classics, London

Schroeder D (2012) Human rights and human dignity: An appeal to separate the conjoined twins. Ethical Theory and Moral Practice 15(3):323–335

Sen A (1992) Missing women. BMJ 304:586–587

Sen A (2003) Missing women – revisited. BMJ 327:1297

Shepherd L (2012) Face to face: a call for radical responsibility in place of compassion. St. John's Law Review 77(3):445–514. http://scholarship.law.stjohns.edu/lawreview/vol77/iss3/1

Singer M (1971) Generalisation in ethics. Russell & Russell, New York

Singer P (1995) Animal liberation. Pimlico, London

Solomon RC (2006) On ethics and living well. Thomson Wadsworth, Belmont CA

South Africa (1996) Constitution of the Republic of South Africa. South African Government. http://www.gov.za/documents/constitution-republic-south-africa-1996

Straits Times (2015) Project Dignity wins social enterprise of the year award. 18 November. http://www.straitstimes.com/singapore/manpower/project-dignity-wins-social-enterprise-of-the-year-award

TASS (2015) Crimea responds with dignity to Ukrainian President's obscene proposal. TASS Russian News Agency, 2 January. http://tass.com/politics/848183

Taylor C (1995) The politics of recognition. In: Philosophical arguments. Harvard University Press, Cambridge MA, p 225–256

The Week Staff (2010) Tsutomu Yamaguchi. The Week, 14 January. http://theweek.com/articles/497706/tsutomu-yamaguchi

Thomas L (1995) Self-respect: theory and practice. In: Dillon RS (ed) Dignity, character and self-respect. Routledge, New York, p 251–270

Tiedemann P (2006) Was ist Menschenwürde? Wissenschaftliche Buchgesellschaft, Darmstadt

Tugendhat E (1993) Vorlesungen über Ethik. Suhrkamp Taschenbuch, Frankfurt

UN (1948) Universal Declaration of Human Rights. United Nations. http://www.un.org/en/universal-declaration-human-rights/

UN (1966) International Covenant on Civil and Political Rights. Adopted by General Assembly resolution 2200A (XXI) of 16 December. Available at http://www.ohchr.org/en/professionalinterest/pages/ccpr.aspx

Vacco v. Quill (nd) Oyez. Chicago-Kent College of Law at Illinois Tech. https://www.oyez.org/cases/1996/95-1858

Vautier B Holly (1996) 'Definitions of Death'. In: Dignity and dying: a Christian appraisal. Eerdmans, Grand Rapids MI, p 96–104. http://www.theologymatters.com/Mayjun97.PDF. Accessed: 13 Dec 2016

Vukadinovich D, Krinsky S (2001) Ethics and law in modern medicine: hypothetical case studies. Springer Science+Business Media, Dordrecht

Waldron J (2015) Dignity, rank, and rights. Oxford, Oxford University Press, Oxford

Washington v. Glucksberg (nd) Oyez. Chicago-Kent College of Law at Illinois Tech https://www.oyez.org/cases/1996/96-110

Wetlesen J (1999) The moral status of beings who are not persons. Environmental Values 8 (3):287–323

Widdecombe A (2010) Strictly for fun. Radio Times, 18–24 September, p 27

Wood A (1999) Kant's ethical thought. Cambridge University Press, Cambridge

Wood A (2008) Human dignity, right and the realm of ends. Acta Juridica i:47–65

Woolhead G, Calnan M, Dieppe P, Tadd W (2004) Dignity in older age: what do older people in the United Kingdom think? Age and Ageing 33(2)165–170

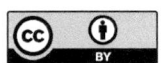

Chapter 3
Dignity in the Middle East

Abstract What is dignity from a Middle Eastern perspective? This chapter is an interpretation of dignity in Islam. To facilitate understanding of the dignity analysis, a short summary of Islam precedes the main discussion, which focuses on the relationships of dignity and power, and dignity and freedom.

Keywords Dignity · Middle east · Freedom · Power · Tawheed

3.1 Islam: A Brief Overview of a World Religion

All major religions make prescriptions about what is wrong and what is right, and all major religions refer to sacred texts (Weitz 2011: 13, 16, 18). Religions are teachings about life.

It is generally agreed that there are five world religions: Christianity with around 2.2 billion believers, Islam with 1.4 billion, Hinduism with 900 million, Buddhism[1] with 500 million, and the smallest world religion, Judaism, with 15 million believers (Gaede 2012). Islam is the second largest world religion, with the highest numbers of believers in Indonesia (200 million), followed by Pakistan (174 million), India (160 million), Bangladesh (145 million), Egypt (78 million) and then Turkey and Iran (both 73 million) (Halm 2011: 7).

Islam is also the youngest world religion. Yet the speed of its development, as well as its considerable geographical expansion, is an extraordinary phenomenon, even on a world scale (Lanczkowski 1989: 169). Originating with the prophet Mohammed in Mecca and Medina (more below), Islam took less than 200 years to spread to the South of France and well into today's Russia.

---

[1]One could argue that Buddhism is not a religion but a way of life and philosophy. According to this understanding, the work of Buddhism is 'not one of generating eternal and absolute answers to ultimate questions, but something much more modest and situationally specific. Most simply, it is the work of disclosing the root conditions of currently experienced trouble or suffering and providing guidance in resolutely dissolving them' (Hershock 2003)

© The Author(s) 2017
D. Schroeder and A. Bani-Sadr, *Dignity in the 21st Century*,
SpringerBriefs in Philosophy, DOI 10.1007/978-3-319-58020-3_3

Christianity, Islam and Judaism are related religions; not only do they share their strong belief in monotheism, but they have early prophets (Halm 2011: 13),[2] such as Abraham, in common and a geographically similar area of origin (Weitz 2011: 25f). According to some scholars, Islam developed in the context of Christianity and Judaism, but combined existing and new elements with such 'genius' (Reuter 2012: 89) that a powerful world religion was born. For instance, Judaism has strong rituals and rules to give believers strength, but no mission. Access to the kingdom of believers is usually only by birth. Christianity, on the other hand, is highly mission-based and access is straightforward. On the other hand, the everyday life of Christians is not rigidly regulated by rituals and prescriptions.

Islam provides rituals and prescriptions and is open to everybody in a way that is not possible in Christianity and Judaism. (Regarding the simplicity of the Muslim confession of faith or credo, see below.)

3.1.1 The Prophet

Prophets have the task of guiding humanity through the messages they receive from God. In the case of Islam, the messages come from Allâh, which means 'God' in Arabic. The founder of Islam is the prophet Mohammed, who first received the words of God through the Archangel Gabriel. The name Mohammed is Arabic for 'praised' of 'praiseworthy'. For Muslims, Mohammed is not just one in a long series of prophets: he is the last prophet, the seal of the prophets (*châyam an-nabiyyîn*) (Halm 2011: 12).

Details about the life of Mohammed have survived to the present day only through documents written after Mohammed's death. The oldest biography of Mohammed was written by Muhammad ibn Ishâg, who was born in Medina in 706 (Halm 2011: 16). The date of Mohammed's death is relatively uncontentious (8 June 632 CE), while the date of his birth is contested and ranges from 552 to 570 CE (Reuter 2012: 82; Armstrong 2001: 3). It is not disputed that he was born in Mecca as part of the Quraysh, the most powerful tribe in the city.

Mohammed never knew his father, who died around the time of his birth, and also lost his mother relatively early. She was buried when he was six, but even before then, he was taken away from her and raised first by a grandfather, then by an uncle (Reuter 2012: 83). As a young man, he accompanied his uncle on his camel trains (caravans) and thus met his first wife, Khadija, a rich, older business woman whom he married when he was 25. Through his marriage, he achieved financial independence (Halm 2011: 19). They were married for 24 years, until Khadija died, leaving him with four daughters, two sons having died in infancy. It

---

[2]However, in Islam a prophet cannot be the son of God, so Jesus is a prophet for Muslims, but not the son of God.

was during his marriage to Khadija that he became a prophet who heard the words of God through the Archangel Gabriel.

> In 610 Common Era, an Arab businessman had an experience that changed the history of the world. Every year ..., Muhammad ibn Abdallah used to retire to a cave on the summit of Mount Hira, just outside Mecca ... where he prayed, fasted and gave alms to the poor. ... Mecca had become a thriving mercantile city, but in the aggressive stampede for wealth some of the old tribal values had been lost. Instead of looking after the weaker members of the tribe ... the Quraysh were now intent on making money. ... There was also spiritual restlessness in Mecca. (Armstrong 2001: 3)

According to historical documents, Mohammed waited (Armstrong 2001: 3) for three years (Reuter 2012: 86) before he offered the words of God to the public. Only Khadija knew of his experience early on, and she became his first believer. When Mohammed went public with his experiences, the citizens of Mecca were not very impressed. Too many self-proclaimed prophets were preaching in the city. However, Mohammed was unlike any of them: the poetic melody of his prophesies and the magic of his words were apparently unsurpassed (Reuter 2012: 87). Still today, many non-Arabic Muslims learn to recite the Koran in Arabic, because of the poetic beauty of the language. It is also said that many converts to Islam were drawn to it when they first heard the text being read out loud (Esposito 2011: 10).

When Mohammed's wife Khadija and his uncle Abû Tâlib died in 619, his position in Mecca became precarious. He started negotiations with two tribes from Yathrib, a city 350 kilometres north-west of Mecca. Yathrib later became known as Medina, short for Madînat an-Nabî, which means 'the city of the prophet'. In 622 the migration (hidjra) of Mohammed and his followers to Medina was completed. Later, the year of the migration was pronounced to be the starting point of the Islamic calendar.

In Medina, Mohammed increased his influence by mediating between the tribes, and over the next ten years he built the foundation of an Islamic state (Halm 2011: 18–21). At the same time, military battles took place between Medina and Mecca over several years. Yet in 630, before his death in 632, Mohammed was able to return to his home town of Mecca, where tribes including the Qurayish accepted the Koran as their sacred text and agreed to become Muslims (Halm 2011: 20).

3.1.2 The Koran and the Hadîths

The Koran (or qur'ān) is the sacred text of Islam, the message of God revealed through the prophet Mohammed. The word means 'reading' or 'recitation' in Arabic. The Koran consists of 114 individual texts called 'surahs' and around 77,000 words. Thus, it is much shorter than, for instance, the New Testament with 181,000 words (Sinai 2012: 11). Rather than being structured according to topics, the Koran is structured according to surah length, with the longer surahs at the beginning and the shorter ones at the end. Citation is usually by surah and verse (e.g. 97: 2). The longest surah contains 286 verses, of which some contain more than 20 words (Sinai 2012: 12). By the time the prophet Mohammed died in 632, he had received the entire text of the Koran, but it was only collected and put into written form after his death (Sinai 2012: 13).

> For Muslims, Muhammad was neither the author nor editor of the Quran. Therefore, the Quran is the eternal, literal word of God, preserved in the original Arabic language. … Many Muslims experience deep aesthetic pleasure from listening to the rich, resonant, rhyming prose, with its repetitions and subtle inflections. (Esposito 2011: 10f)

Islam does not rely solely on the revelations captured in the Koran. A second foundation on which the religion is built is the life of the prophet. For Muslims, the prophet was the ideal Muslim (Halm 2011: 43; Weitz 2011: 79). His life served and continues to serve as an example to all believers. What he said during his lifetime forms the *hadîths*, the prophet's sayings. Most of the *hadîths* cover questions of right and wrong and also form the basis of Islamic law (*sharî'a*).[3] In the everyday life of a Muslim, the *hadîths* are often seen as highly important (Halm 2011: 43).

3.1.3 Islam in Everyday Life

The term 'Muslim' comes from the Arabic and means 'one who surrenders and submits to God'. By surrendering to God, one can achieve peace, according to the Koran (Weitz 2011: 75). Muslim life is based on five pillars or obligations. Here we will describe the obligations for Sunni Muslims, the largest branch of Islam.

The first is the confession of faith or credo (*shahâda*). In a two-part formula, every Muslim must express the fundamental belief that there is no god but God and that Mohammed is the prophet of God. Conversion to Islam is an easy, informal act. All that is required is to say the confession of faith in an honest spirit (Weitz 2011: 63).

The second obligation is the prayer ritual. Prayer consists of a range of movements that have to be performed five times a day (Weitz 2011: 63). Before praying, the believer has to perform a ritual cleansing. When praying, the believer has to face towards the Kaaba in Mecca, the most sacred site in Islam. This was introduced by Mohammed in the 18th month after his arrival in Medina. Before this change, prayers were made facing Jerusalem (Reuter 2012: 89).

The third obligation for any Muslim is the fasting at *Ramadân*, commemorating the month when Mohammed received the first revelation. *Ramadân* is always the ninth month of the Islamic moon calendar. Since the moon calendar is shorter than the 365-day sun calendar, the date of *Ramadân* always changes. The fasting requires that the believer take no food or fluid while the sun is up. There are exceptions for children and those who are ill, pregnant or very old, but otherwise the fasting rule applies to everybody. Of course fasting in winter is much less burdensome than fasting in summer. *Ramadân* lasts for one month.

---

[3]This brief introduction to Islam will not look into the Islamic legal system.

The fourth obligation is alms for the poor. The community of muslims (*umma*) is a solidarity collective, and the affluent have to help the poor. The Koran does not stipulate an exact sum or percentage of income that needs to be donated, but a general rule of 10% has been established (Halm 2011: 71).

The fifth obligation is the pilgrimage to Mecca. Those who are privileged enough to be able to afford this journey (sometimes a village will save money so that one villager can go) are required to walk around the Kaaba seven times, as the main pilgrimage ritual (Halm 2011: 75).

Not only has Islam been unusually fast and successful historically in spreading its message, but today, at the beginning of the 21st century, it is the fastest growing of all world religions (with a 1.84% growth rate between 2000 and 2005) (Admin 2007).

What follows is an introduction to an understanding of human dignity in the Koran. It includes brief parallels with the Western understanding of dignity.

3.2 Introduction to Dignity in the Koran

According to the Koran,[4] everything created is noble and dignified (Koran 17:70; 42:7; 31:10). The dignity of each and every living phenomenon emanates from and is connected to intelligent life itself (Koran 21:26−27; 49:13). This pronouncement from the Koran is reminiscent of both the Catholic belief that dignity is God-given and the Kantian belief that dignity is irrevocably linked to rationality.

Because of their dignity, all persons are free and, as long as they are not neglectful of God, they are also noble. One achieves this nobility in three steps:

- First by willingly enduring trial (*ebtelaa*) (Koran 89:15).
- Second by refusing to submit to the law of force (Koran 25:25).
- Third by recognising the nobility of all phenomena and the dignity of all creation, *including one's own self-worth* (Koran 17:23; 89:17−18, emphasis added).

Humans become and remain noble through virtuous acts (Koran 49:13), and virtue is realised both in the expansion of freedom through development (Koran 72:14) and by excelling in learning, justice, service for others and friendship (Bani-Sadr 1992: 1371). This reference to the Koran and its interpretation are strongly reminiscent of the Western understanding of dignity as a virtue.

Furthermore, in Islam, human dignity increases as we honour each individual and encourage them to increase their own dignity. For this reason, it is stated in the Koran that there is no compulsion in religion. Religion is a method of

---

[4]All verses from the Koran are from the 1946 English translation by Abdullah Yusuf Ali, available at https://archive.org/details/HolyQurAnYusufAliTranslation1946Edition_201508 or http://www.islam101.com/quran/yusufAli/.

'deviolentisation', a way of removing the role of force from society and replacing humiliation with dignity. In other words, nobility is an attribute of God and, like any other of God's attributes, it exists in human beings. The Catholic equivalent formulation is that human beings are created in the image of God.

God's gift to humans—indeed to all creatures—is that they are created free and with dignity. We can see this in the story of human creation as told in the Koran. Here, God informs the angels that a successor (a vicegerent) will be created on earth. For a Catholic this may sound like a reference to a prophet such as Jesus, but the story in the Koran talks about human beings as successors and vicegerents, not a single prophet. The story says that the angels asked God 'will you place therein one who will make mischief and shed blood?'. God replied 'I know what you know not' (Koran 2:30). From the Koranic perspective, history is a successive cycle of alienation and awakening; one group of people strays from its own human nature (*fetrah*), leading to its destruction and that of its environment; another takes up the torch and becomes conscious of its humanity and tries to reverse the destruction.

Historical process, therefore, is a process of development, and human dignity is forged as some awakened human beings assume roles of leadership in it. However, it often happens that people are alienated in power relations and become instruments of destructive power. Nevertheless, as the process of history is a movement from decay to development, whenever one group of people moves towards demise, another will rise to revolution and open the horizon for human development (Koran 6:129−134, 164−165; 7:69, 129; 10:13, 14, 73; 11:50−57; 24:55; 16:59−62). Even when an entire nation begins to decay, there are some individuals who live in freedom, enhance their dignity (their nobility and their virtue), and create a new revolution that paves the way for human freedom and development. By standing for the right and the good, they become God's vicegerents on earth (Koran 10:70−82).

What differentiates the path of life from the path of death and destruction? We must remember that only the free human is noble; therefore human dignity is contingent upon the recognition of one's own nobility (self-worth) and others' nobility. Neglect of others' dignity is a result of the neglect of one's own. This is similar to Kant's views on dignity, as he emphasises that one has obligations to oneself to uphold one's dignity as well as an obligation to others to respect theirs. The neglect of one's own and others' dignity grows out of submission to force. When force becomes universal, corruption also becomes universal (Koran 24:18; 89:12). In other words, violence—including violence in the form of extreme poverty—can destroy life and environment.

When a people submits to force, its members also start to perceive themselves as objects. Again, one can observe a similarity to Kant's Formula of Humanity, which forbids seeing and treating other people solely as means to one's own ends. Arrogance based on power breeds opportunities for humiliation, just as superiority necessitates inferiority, for power does not exist without destruction. This not only means that when one strives for superiority others must be humiliated; worse, in humiliating others one loses one's own dignity by becoming an instrument of, and indeed synonymous with, power and force itself. A person who seeks superiority in this way has already become inferior. Hence, liberation from universal humiliation, violence and poverty can only be accomplished by recognising one's *fetrah*, or human nature, and believing that 'never will Allah change the condition of a people until they change it themselves' (Koran 13:11). If we achieve this, then we can revolutionise ourselves and realise the dignity which is unique to us—unique because humans have accepted God's 'trust' (Koran 33:72).

This trust to which the Koran refers is nothing but the responsibility of leadership towards development and freedom (Bani-Sadr 1992). By assuming this responsibility, we not only develop ourselves, but also undertake the development of our environment, both of which can only be realised in freedom. This stands in opposition to the growth of power, which only increases violence, destruction, poverty and inequality. The process of development should be seen as a single process; hence, there is no development if one section of the human community becomes rich while another becomes poor, or if some increase their wealth at the expense of the environment. This is rather a process of enslavement to the laws of power. Therefore what distinguishes living in freedom from living towards death and destruction is the absence of compulsion. If human beings neglect their responsibility as God's worldly vicegerents, they will not only lead the world to destruction; at this point, they become depleted of dignity.

As mentioned above, people are born with *fetrah*, and as a result they are endowed with divine attributes. One such attribute is *tawheed*, or holistic unity. This central attribute, the core of human nature, also functions as a guiding principle for living.[5] The loss or forgetting of this attribute leads to the emergence of belief systems which are based on dichotomies, ways of seeing the world which polarise rather than unite. This is the meaning of *kofr*, or blasphemy—it is the ultimate loss of dignity (Koran 35:39). God's warning is thus clear: blasphemy is nothing but forgetting that we are God's vicegerents on earth, the neglect of our own freedom and loss of our own nobility, becoming wretched, and causing harm to ourselves and others (Koran 10:26−27).

3.3 Dignity and Power

As noted earlier, historical processes are characterised by the recurring demise of groups which succumb to blasphemy and the subsequent rise of others which strive to honour human dignity. However, according to the Koran, it is *tawheed* that will ultimately be the destiny of humankind. Right will replace falsity and people will

---

[5]*Tawheed* can be defined as a lack of separation in everything existing, a unity of 'self' and 'other', 'individual' and 'society', God and human, human and environment. This concept disrupts all these dichotomies and makes them 'untrue'. Ali Shariati defines it as a world view which sees the 'whole universe as a unity, instead of dividing it into this world and the hereafter, the natural and the supernatural, substance and meaning, spirit and body. It means regarding the whole of existence as a single form, a single living and conscious organism, possessing will, intelligence, feeling and purpose' (Shariati 1979: 82).

genuinely become God's vicegerents on earth (Koran 24:18, 55).[6] This principle refers not only to the past, but to the future as well. How do we know this? How do we know that life will continue so that believers can fulfil this role?

Initially, according to the Koran, humans were created from a mud which contained all the ingredients of life, into which God blew spirit (Koran 55:14; 32:7–10). Human *fetrah* became godlike, and the *fetrah* was *tawheed* (Koran 30:30),[7] in the best proportions and most beautiful (Koran 95:4; 82:7; 64:3), and God congratulated himself on this creation (Koran 23:12–14). Life could not emerge without *tawheed*; Imam Ali once said that human beings are microcosms of the entire universe. God created humans and other living beings with dignity and called upon humans to uphold this dignity. Humans volunteered to assume this responsibility, while other living beings did not. However, if in time God's earth is not to be depleted of vicegerents, there must be people to carry out the responsibility of acting in this capacity.

> We did indeed offer the Trust to the Heavens and the Earth and the Mountains; but they refused to undertake it, being afraid thereof; but Man undertook it – he was indeed unjust and foolish. (Koran 33:72)

Acting in the capacity of vicegerents is only possible if humans accept the responsibility of trust, with their entire being (Koran 17:36), a kind of leadership that reflects and guarantees the continuation of this responsibility. In order to assume it, human beings need a spiritual dimension: they have to develop their abilities, and actively and continuously strive for improvement. Only in this context can we see the importance of leading ourselves and others. We have been given divine attributes to be able to assume this responsibility. The Koran explains that God taught humans—both non-believers and believers—the names of these attributes (Koran 2:31), as well as the ability to speak and to write (Koran 96:4−5; 55:3; 2:282). God gave human beings the talent of seeking knowledge, intelligence and wisdom, and the ability to become conscious of themselves and distinguish between good and evil.

'We have shown him the sign of ourselves so he begins to reflect' (Koran 76:2; 75:14; 57:17). God has also given human beings talents such as innovation, creativity and industry. But some people became passive and some became active; in other words, some used their talents for development and others, through resorting to lies, deception and force, destroyed them (Koran 21:80; 16:76; 7:191; 29:17). God also gave humans a nature which seeks justice and showed them the way towards it (Koran 4:135; 42:15). God gave humans the talent of leadership, creating us as free and goal-oriented (Bani-Sadr 1992), so that people could distinguish between development and mutiny (Koran 2:256). This guidance was given to both believers and non-believers, and God warns that all those who stray from the path

---

[6]'Allah has promised, to those among you who believe and work righteous deeds, that He will, of a surety, grant them in the land, inheritance (of power), as He granted it to those before them.'

[7]Imam Hassan, the second Shia imam, stated that God here specifies that *fetrah* is *tawheed*; thus, humans must be free.

of development will inevitably lead lives of greed, excess and ultimately destruction and death (Koran 76:3; 96:6).

Despite these gifts, human beings are imperfect. They can become alienated from their *fetrah* and weak and restless (Koran 4:28; 70:19). As noted earlier, humans generally fall into two groups: one that develops its talents, and another that destroys them by resorting to force and deception (Koran 21:80; 16:76; 7:191; 29:17). If one stays steadfast in *fetrah*, weaknesses will become strengths and dignity will be increased. However, if perspectives shift away from *tawheed*, life forces will become transformed into forces of death, leading to tyranny, death and destruction.

The Koranic explanation of human alienation reminds us of a fact we often ignore, namely that human rights are intrinsic to human beings. Each person, as a vicegerent of God, is born free, born a leader. Before human beings assume any belief (religious or otherwise), they have rights and a responsibility to defend these rights, as well as those of any other person irrespective of belief, race, nationality, ethnicity and so on. In other words, rights are not given to people through agreements among humans; we are born with them. This is in line with the interpretation of dignity as an intrinsic property for rational beings, leading to rights, as in Kant; and for all human beings, as God's gift, as in Catholicism. In Islam, one cannot gain or lose rights by believing or disbelieving in any specific belief system, including Islam. There is no compulsion in religion (Koran 2:256). A person has, among other rights, the right to turn towards religion.

However, a Koranic lesson that is highly important is this. So long as people want to remain free and are conscious of their freedom, it is impossible for a power to emerge that would lead to the loss of freedom and rights. Such a power emerges when people become alienated and forget freedom, rights and dignity. No one can revoke one's dignity but oneself, and only when one defends rights does one become God's vicegerent on earth. Like many constitutions around the world, the Koran claims that dignity is inviolable and already embedded in human nature, as noted by Abraham (Koran 16:120−123), who spoke on behalf of humanity. In defending dignity and rights, humans are never alone; God is always with us, and we will emerge victorious in the end.

But why are freedom and rights intrinsic in human beings? Neither can be defined by any principle other than *tawheed*. In this context, some would argue that one person's freedom begins where another's ends. However, if this defines freedom, can we argue that every individual's knowledge stops where another's starts, or that one person's creativity ends where another's begins? Or can we argue that our talents for justice, friendship and love end where those of others start? If we argue this way, we can see that power is embedded in this definition of freedom, as without it we cannot say that one freedom ends where another begins. Force is the absence of freedom. Hence, if we reduce freedom to exercise force, then each individual becomes a prisoner of the freedom of others, and relations become power relations. It is obvious in this case that the stronger will violate the freedom of the weak. Within power relations, freedom, human rights, human life and nature become casualties.

However, if we see freedom and rights based on the principles of *tawheed*, we can sense that freedom; it is a freedom that the intellect feels at the moment of creativity, at the moment we become one with intelligent life. This is why any ideas which are devoid of force become 'free'. Thus, not only can freedom not be limited; it furthermore removes limits and boundaries; it is not the limit of another's freedom, but its extension.

What are the freedoms that God's generosity has given us?

3.4 Dignity and Freedom

With dignity, God has also given human beings freedoms (Fig. 3.1).

1. The freedom to choose one's guiding principles. No one can be forced to accept the guiding principles of power. This freedom can be linked to the Kantian foundation of dignity, namely the human intellect's power to be self-legislative.
2. The freedom to choose goals.
3. The freedom to choose to establish free relations. If one does not want to enter into power relations with others and nature, no one from outside can force a human being to do so. Even while immersed in fire, Abraham did not lose the freedom of his intellect, and instead used it to turn the fire cold. As long as one does not enter into the closed circuit of power, one can preserve freedom of the intellect, establish free relations with those who function within power relations, remain free, help others become conscious of their freedom, and indeed become prophets of freedom.
4. The freedom to choose information, ideas and discourses (whether of power or freedom).
5. The freedom to attain knowledge. Learning is a human talent, and a human right.

Fig. 3.1 Freedoms deriving from dignity

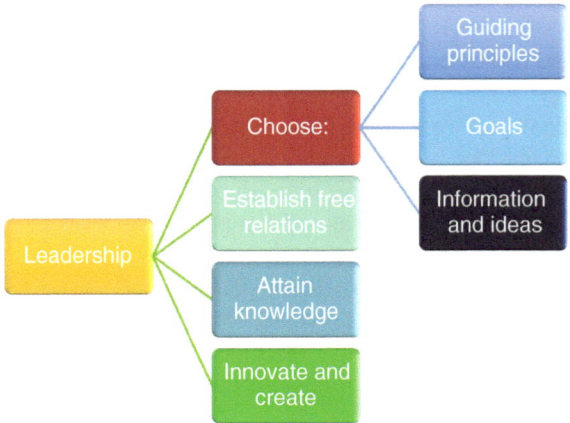

6. The freedom to innovate, invent and create. No one can be deprived of this freedom, as it, like life itself, is limitless, and the human intellect feels this freedom at the moment of creativity.
7. The freedom of leadership, which coordinates the activities of all other human talents according to certain guiding principles. No one can externally deprive a person of the talent of leadership and freedom of action so long as this is not desired. If God wanted to guide everyone he would do so (Koran 32:13; 28:56; 27:81, 92; 30:53; 2:276), but human beings have the freedom and ability to guide themselves.

Other human talents, such as love, art and economy (which coordinates other talents in the process of development) are also internal freedoms. There is a misconception that power can give or take freedom, but this could not be further from the truth. Only when people are addicted to force can they become neglectful of freedoms. Freedom is intrinsic to life and cannot be given or taken. To explain this, we know that 'negative freedom' is understood as an open domain for thought, expression and action. Since power can close this circuit, it has been believed that power can grant and remove freedom. However, it was through God's generosity that this domain became infinite and the discourse of freedom became the method of development in freedom. Hence, when confronted with force, God has to remember his generosity and use a method for eliminating force. God has to protect internal freedom, that limitless freedom which is the lack of compulsion, and prevent us from being alienated in the closed domain of force.

For instance, the closed circuit of compulsion which has created racial, ethnic and national borders was born out of neglect of the fact that all humans share a common nature. Addiction to power has made us forget this, and if humans do not heed their nature, their ever-increasing production and consumption of violence will endanger human and natural life alike. It is only through the process of accepting this common human nature that an individual will accept that s/he is equal with others, and that all these apparent differences, including differences of religion, are only matters of identification.

Humans all share the same precious nature. Take, for example, the Koranic explanation for gender equality. After Adam was banished from Heaven, he repented. As a result, neither men nor women are born sinners. Until the advent of Islam, however, women were perceived as subhuman and the source of men's deception in the Garden of Eden. The Koran challenged this view and argued that men and women were equal. It argued that men and women shared the same soul (Koran 4:1; 36:36); that they were from one another, and that the one was the other. At the same time, the Koran noted that they had different virtues. For instance, until then, women had been perceived in philosophical and religious belief as the source of corruption and death. However, the Koran recognises the following virtues in women:

1. A woman is a *kosar*[8] and farm of life (Koran 108; 2:223); a farm which never becomes arid as long as she lives in harmony with her nature. On this farm, seeds are planted with love, and fruit ripens and is cultivated in love.
2. A woman is a teacher of love. She turns marriage to the centre of love and prevents men from going astray in animosity, to return to the farm of love (Koran 30:21; 7:189).
3. God created women as artists: they have the ability to transcend domains which are limited by different dominant beliefs at different times. According to the Koran, throughout time, women played a key role in the transition from old eras to new. That, it says, is the artistry of women. Kaaba (in Mecca) is the holiest place for Muslims; all pray towards it. A slave woman named Hajar is buried in its centre. She gave a child to Abraham in his old age (Koran 37:109) and, with the love of motherhood, brought water from the burning sands of the desert to a spring which still flows. This fountain is a sign of the continuity of life. In another example, Moses' mother gave her son to the water and the Pharaoh's wife rescued him. Moses was raised in the palace of the Pharaoh, who had ordered his soldiers to kill all male infant Jews (Koran 28:7−8). Mary gave birth to Jesus without a husband (Koran 3:45−48; 23:50), and Mohammad sought solace from the anxiety and burden of the responsibility of prophecy in the arms of Khadija, his first wife. It was thus a statement of fact when he said that 'Khadija was half the prophecy'.
4. Women have the excellence of motherhood. The Koran reminds children to increase their respect for their mothers (Koran 31:14) and the Prophet stated that paradise is under the feet of mothers.
5. Women are an indicator and reminder of men's dignity. The inferiority of women in societies is a sign of social decadence. Honouring women is the sign of a healthy society and of men's dignity. However, it is a woman's job to protect her dignity by elevating her dignity and calling to men to recognise her and all creation (Koran 2:237).

Men also have virtues, which combine themselves with women's; justice is the criterion which regulates this combination. Here are men's virtues, as combined with women's virtues:

1. The excellence of fatherhood, when combined with the excellence of motherhood, will develop the talent of leadership and widen the space for development even further.
2. The virtue of consistency and ability to trust from time to time may be undermined in men. Hence, when the ability of a woman to reproduce this confidence in a man becomes intertwined with a man's excellence, it will lead to a lasting love relationship.

---

[8]Mohammed was at one time called *aptar*, signifying that he would leave no lineage because he had no son. On the other hand, *kosar*, a female adjective, signifies the opposite: that a woman will bear many children. *Kosar* can also be defined as a fountain or stream in which God's virtue flows. Here the two definitions are interrelated, implying that God's virtues in fact live through women.

3. A woman is the measure of generosity, and a man by honouring this generosity in women will remain in touch with his own dignity. In other words, by their very existence women remind men of their dignity. It is in this context we can see that 'virtue' means the recognition of each other's dignity. Hence, any attempt to increase women's dignity also increases men's dignity. Consequently, the composition of these excellences in men and women, by honouring other created beings, will increase the element of dignity throughout creation.

4. Women are teachers of love, and one of men's virtues is to defend women's freedom and independence against violation. However, the prime defenders of this are women themselves. The combination of these two talents will make the family the centre of mutual trust and love, and will remove force from human relations (Koran 2:237): 'And do not forget Liberality between yourselves. For God sees well All that ye do.'

Hence, drawing a strict boundary between women's and men's excellences would not only make their combination impossible; it would also indicate a neglect of both male and female excellences. It follows that when marriage is not based on the combination of a woman's and man's talents, then power relations will dictate the terms of the relationship. Not only this, but love and friendship will then be marginalised in such a relationship; in fact, it will turn marriage into a power-producing arrangement which will destroy the relationship.

Here it seems necessary to mention that according to the Koran, Satan was the first being who, through belief in power, saw himself as superior to humans by referring to the differences between human beings and himself (Koran 7:12): '(God) said, "What prevented Thee from bowing down When I commanded thee?" He said: "I am better than He: Thou didst create Me from fire, and him from clay."'

God therefore asked people not to follow Satan and his belief in power, and not to establish boundaries based on gender, race, ethnicity or nation, and reminded them that God had created them in different colours and no colour had superiority over the others: 'And among His Signs is the creation of the heavens and the earth, the variations in your languages and your colours: verily in that are Signs for those who know' (Koran 30:22). After all, the sole reason for placing people in tribes and nations was so that they could recognise one another: 'O mankind! We created you from a single (pair) of a male and female, and made you into nations and tribes, that ye may know each other. Verily the most honoured of you in the sight of God is (he who is) the most righteous of you. And God has full knowledge and is well acquainted (with all things)' (Koran 49:13).

Therefore, to live in freedom means to be equal in regard to rights, duties and participation in the responsibility of leadership, irrespective of race or financial status. It is important to notice that prior to the Koran, in various philosophical and religious beliefs, justice was defined on the basis of inequalities. The Koran, however, defines justice as a line which separates 'beings', or the freely created, from 'non-beings', which are products of force. To explain this, we need to know that 'force' by its nature is not only incapable of constructing, but in fact tends to destruct whatever it interacts with. Therefore any inequality in the domain of politics, economy, culture and society is a product of force and leads to the destruction of people, other creatures and nature. However, different but compatible characteristics, such as excellences in men and women, indicate equality between the pairs, as they share the same origin (Bani-Sadr 1992). The only time acquired inequalities may be seen in the context of justice is when they are a result of competition between people in terms of leadership, knowledge, justice, service, or training of the body, mind and spirit (Bani-Sadr 1992). Moreover, those who win such a race should not only refrain from using their privileged position to dominate others and create inequalities, but also realise that their dignity depends on having regard for others' dignity by helping them towards self-improvement. The combination of succeeding in such competition and living in dignity will make the 'winners' forecasters (Koran 35:19−24); role models and *imams* (leaders) of development for those who have fallen behind. Such dynamism creates a process, a movement, from inequality to equality in an open horizon of spirituality (Bani-Sadr 1992).

3.5 How Dignity Becomes Realisable

To ensure a better understanding of what dignity means in Islam, we now discuss the type of honour (*takrim*) which increases dignity.

God has created enough of everything in nature (Koran 54:49); it is humans who create scarcity. The question is, how? The answer: they forget their dignity and that of all creation. As a result, they transform non-material needs into material ones, authenticate force and turn this force into the basis for their relationships with themselves, others and nature. This is accomplished in the following way.

Natural needs cannot be realised by the consumption of unnatural products. The human body has certain needs, but the products which one uses to satisfy those needs should not create a power relation within the body. Hence, the production and consumption of products which have destructive effects on the body are a result of the neglect of dignity (Koran 5:90−91; 2:173; 6:145). Furthermore, the Koran emphasises and encourages thinking people to notice that when the principle of dichotomy becomes the guiding principle of thought and action, then the open circuit of material↔spiritual will be transformed into a closed circuit of material↔material. In this closed circuit, even spiritual needs have to be realised through material ones, and as non-material needs become material, their realisation only becomes possible through mass production and consumption. As a result, as these needs increase, natural resources decrease.

For example, the love between man and woman is spiritual, as the right to love is a spiritual love. However, if love becomes alienated in 'sheer lust', then the element of 'time', which is infinite in love, becomes finite in lust. As the needs of love are realisable through non-material and spiritual means, the needs for sheer lust are only realisable through material production. Hence, such needs have to be constantly renewed. Therefore, the closed circuit of material↔material production and consumption is accompanied by waste and dissipation (Koran 17:53; 6:121; 4:76). Since it is impossible for everyone to participate in the competition for mass consumption, poverty is constantly increasing, both in human communities and in the natural environment. Hence, we are observing the erosion of human communities, the great majority of them by poverty and a small minority by mass consumption.

Certain methods for harmonising material and spiritual needs were recommended at a time when the communities on the Arabian Peninsula were living in poverty. The teachings noted that any consumption which negatively affects the natural balance of the body and deranges the mind is wastefully extravagant and fatal. It taught people that if they do not try to develop and actualise their talents, the energy used for these talents cannot stay unoccupied and hence will be used for domination and transgression (Koran 96:6). However, the question is: how do we know that we are on the path to development and not domination (and *fozoon talabi* or greed)? There are 14 ways to measure this.

1. Human development should be accompanied by the prosperity of nature. Hence, any development which is accompanied by environmental destruction should not be seen as development but an act of dominance and greed, which eventually will lead both humans and the environment to the valley of death. According to the Koran, the elimination of ethnic groups and cities resulted from their deviation from the path of development.[9]

There are two approaches to the relationship between human beings and their environment. One perceives nature as an active entity and humans as passive subordinates to nature, and the other sees humans as a dominant entity which has to conquer nature and ferociously exploit its resources for the wholesale consumption of its resources. How is it possible, one can ask, that the Koran provides us with the solution to encroaching environmental disaster, when it was written 1,400 years ago in the deserts of the Arabian Peninsula? How is it possible that such a warning should have come from anyone but God?

2. If a right creates a zero-sum relation in which one will reap benefit at the expense of someone else's loss, then this cannot be seen as a right. Even if a 'right' is seen as an entity which one has and the other does not, this also is not 'right' but falsity. If we can see that human rights are not exercised in their totality in any country, then will it be wrong to assume that the reason for this is that those who are aware of these rights feel themselves to be entitled to them but do not see as their duty the defence of these rights in regard to others? If so, then one can only explain this discrepancy by arguing that the guiding principles of these people's thoughts and actions are based on power relations. On this ground, as pointed out already, there is a zero-sum relationship between self

---

[9]This refers to the destiny of the people of Hud, Thamud and A'ad in the Koran, which is discussed below (see also Bani-Sadr 1992).

rights and other rights. Those whose functioning is based on this principle regard themselves as having a right over animals and nature. However, do such people recognise not only their duty to ensure that nature and animals do not suffer as the result of the exercise of right, but also that it should involve the furthering of natural prosperity? This is not generally the case, precisely because the utilisation of resources can become part of the domain of power relations, and this is inevitably accompanied by destruction.

Why does this happen? In short, because in these relationships humans become negligent of their identity, and consequently do not recognise the dignity surrounding them. However, if they apply the principle of *tawheed*, humans do not perceive themselves to be in opposing relations with other living beings and nature. This view makes it possible to exercise rights, and hence the defence of right becomes one's method for living. Also, one perceives 'duty' solely as the exercise of 'right', and hence any duty which stands outside rights is a commandment of force and will not be obeyed. Finally, one should consider any expediency which stands outside rights as mere corruption, since to exercise such an expediency will violate right in favour of power.

3. Pairs enjoy dignity (Koran 24:26; 42:7). To explain this, we can say that humans are not born in order to spend their time struggling and fighting with each other. Hence, those who use religion as an excuse to dominate others are walking in the path of Satan (Koran 4:76). When the principle of dichotomy replaces that of *tawheed*, people begin to believe that struggle is the basis of life. As a result, a great part of their talents and natural resources is wasted in the production and consumption of violence (e.g. weapons and drugs). The expenditure for wars, all types of wars, destroys natural resources, leads to the expansion of poverty and brings us to the brink of environmental collapse. In order to overcome this, people need to establish relationships based on five principles: the right to participation, the right to differ, the right to friendship, the right of the weak to become able and equal to able people, and, as a result, the right to peace (Fig. 3.2).

Fig. 3.2 Five principles for relationships

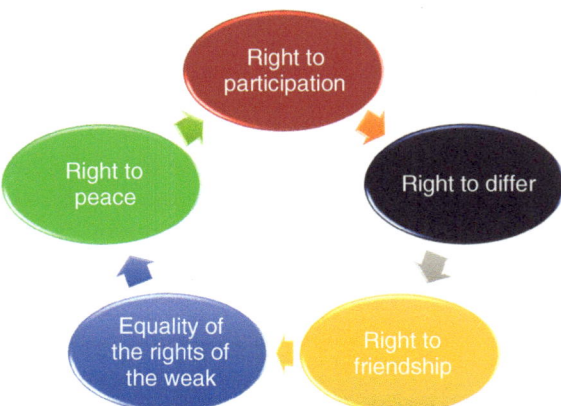

4. When a transparent intellect has transparent goals and methods, it is a 'free intellect'. However, when power becomes the goal, then the intellect will become immersed in ambiguity. As a result of immersion in this increasing darkness, humans become neglectful of their rights and dignity, and those of other created beings. That is why the Koran states that evil will plunge people into darkness and that to turn to God is to come out of this darkness towards the light (Koran 2:257). The Koran is generous in part because it is transparent and free from ambiguity. Furthermore, it is a method for escaping the ambiguity of worshipping power and for entering the lightness of gaining dignity. It is impossible to be transparent when one neglects dignity, freedom and other rights, and when thought, speech and action are based on force. Hence, the only way to realise freedom and human dignity is for thought, speech and action to be entirely clear and transparent.

Since this principle is based on de-violentisation and opening the closed circuit of force into an open circuit characterised by the absence of force and freedom, the Koran says that peace is a blessing. The way to achieve peace is to come out of darkness and into light. Peace increases dignity (Koran 11:52, 53; 4:128; 5:165; 33:44; 25:25, 26). Virtue is achieved by removing all forms of compulsion. Dignity will be realised when virtue is achieved.

5. According to the Koran, Satan was originally an angel who began to discriminate and, as a result, became neglectful of his/her destiny. Any discrimination creates demarcation; each demarcation despises and becomes despised, and hence to demarcate is to lose dignity. To be free from discrimination is to gain dignity. To see oneself as superior or inferior to others comes from losing dignity; however, if you see yourself as superior your dignity suffers less than that of someone who sees him/herself as inferior. This is why forgetting one's abilities is to neglect one's dignity and to become addicted to feeling inferior, which is a greater tyranny (Koran 2:61; 23:27; 30:29, 54; 4:148, 149; 35:10).

6. It has already been mentioned that to honour all created beings absolutely is to add to one's own dignity. The moment of creativity is the moment at which we become one with life. This is when a person will feel the full meaning of authentic freedom. Hence, if people become one with life in their activities and talents and feel that freedom, they live in God, as God's vicegerents, and help others to develop as well as themselves. It is dignity to honour both creator and created (Koran 2:186, 256; 11:97; 72:14).

7. When this occurs, all social institutions, including religious and educational institutions, will have been founded on human dignity and rights. At present, most social institutions and systems are instead based on honouring the structures of power. That is why in our societies there is a constant conflict between dignity, human rights and power, and in this struggle power always wins over human dignity.

It is in this context that aggressive wars and torture, which humiliate humans to an unimaginable level and even lead to their death, are regarded as justified. We have seen this in the execution of hundreds of prisoners at the Qala-i Jangi fortress in Afghanistan, and also in the systematic torture of prisoners at Guantanamo Bay, Abu Ghraib and so on. All are 'justified' with arguments that goals justify means. We are told that the unimaginable torture and humiliation of prisoners—so extreme that even some of the torturers cannot bring themselves to take part in it—are carried out in order to prevent major terrorist acts. But terrorism continues and spreads despite this torture; it will be the shame of human beings in years to come. Now people become spectators to torture and terrorism, despite the fact that they see that these practices are producing social harm and that these methods of torture not only violate human dignity and rights but also contribute to the rise in terrorism. Yet still both the terrorism and the torture continue.

Torture leads to the spread of terrorism. Such methods increase the very thing they are meant to eliminate because their use proves to the people involved that from the state's point of view, power has dignity, not humans. Social groups and even whole societies also start to believe that power and its manifestations (e.g. money) have primary dignity. Hence, these manifestations have become social gods because humans have been devalued and lost their dignity. When humans lose their dignity, then violence inevitably becomes global.

The methods used by the West, especially America's preventive war or the 'fight against terrorism', have led to the spread of terrorism and other types of violence. To break this vicious circle, the only solution is for human dignity to replace power. We need to renew social structures so that they are based on the dignity of rights. We need open social systems that are able to transform; social systems in which human dignity and rights become realities and accumulate in the process of development.

8. To exercise and defend rights increases human dignity. To reconsider truth and to speak it, even if we suffer for it (Koran 4:135), also increases dignity. A human being has the right to know and the right and duty to state the truth. If we do not seek truth and reality, we will become prisoners of a fantasy world and allow ourselves to be manipulated by power and lose our own dignity. That is why to tell the truth before a tyrant—to speak truth to power—is a great jihad (*jihad afzal*), and to tell the truth to oneself, and to remind oneself of rights and duties to exercise these rights is the greatest jihad (*jihad akbar*). Both forms of jihad are attempts to become knowledgeable about one's dignity, to increase it and recognise it in all human beings.

9. When we become cognisant of our dignity, we have an open future (Koran 75:5). More than 40 years ago, Willy Brandt, then Chancellor of Germany, promised that humans would achieve a time of plenty. This was when two competing ideologies—Marxism and liberalism—were each claiming to offer the best prescription for development. However, when one cannot make every moment of the future present, such claims are fantasies created by discourses of power in order to deceive. In other words, if within liberal or Marxist systems it was actually possible to move towards the time of plenty, this possibility should have been experienced more and more every day. However, because both

systems function within the closed circuit of material↔material, both lead to increases in need, so that demand always exceeds supply. We can estimate the use of natural resources and the extent of the damage it is causing to the environment. Hence, I came to the conclusion that both economic systems (capitalism and socialism) make it possible to use up natural resources in advance and by doing so predetermine the future. In other words, by closing off the future, human beings alive today are humiliating themselves. Now we can see that teenagers are fearful of the future, fearful of not finding jobs, fearful that they will have worse lives than their parents. How can politicians, who have become incapable of solving contemporary social problems, talk about solving the future? While we know that the future must be open to exercise dignity, in order to open it we have to replace a closed circuit of material↔material with material↔spirit.

10. There are different points of view about what constitutes dynamic forces, but there is consensus that humans and their guiding principles are the main elements. However, when guiding principles are based on a discourse of power, this leads to the destruction of dynamic forces and the environment. When we look at the contemporary world, we see a sickening form of expertise, and a majority of human communities being deprived of expertise. This is one of the greatest factors in the destruction of dynamic forces. Not only can people without expertise not find jobs, or only find jobs that are incompatible with their human dignity; even those with expertise destroy themselves from within as they have ceased to be whole beings. It is obvious that they become neglectful of their dignity and rights. To explain this, currently expertise—one of many human talents—dominates the entire domain of time, mind and action, the entire being. As a result, other talents do not have the opportunity to develop, and this starts to destroy the expert from within, making him/her an instrument of power.

In contemporary societies, people are at the service of power. That is why those lacking expertise do not have the opportunity to develop a talent which will make them experts. It is obvious, when seven billion people, each of whom is a collection of talents, do not have the opportunity to coordinate their talents, that these talents can only be used in destruction. One can then only ask how much damage is done to humans and the environment due to the loss of opportunity for development. I know that some people talk about changing the structure of labour, but the realisation of the perfect human[10] (which will be realised when humans are able to free themselves from being a labour force to be sold) is only to be achieved either when the ideal society is established or when the hours of labour are decreased and leisure time increased. Some even talk about changing the structure of labour in a way that would make it possible for people to participate directly in the leadership of society. Modern theories of social justice draw links between labour and human dignity. However, as it is a fact that humans are collections of talents, the structure

---

[10]In other words, a fully developed person with fully developed talents.

of labour should be arranged to embrace all types of labour which are responsive to these talents. This, though, has not attracted much attention. It is obvious that within the principle of power it is impossible to imagine a person as a collection of talents, let alone suggest an open social system which is transformative and in harmony with human development. The truth is, the structure of labour in any society indicates the direction towards which dynamic forces are activated, and this direction tells us the measure of collective consciousness in regard to human dignity.

11. The spreading of poverty, people, nature, disease, financial corruption, the drug trade, and social crises and ills at a global level is a product of relations of domination. All these are legitimised, to varying degrees, within discourses of power. This reveals that the common denominator of discourses of power is a belief in the inability of humans to participate in social leadership, the assumption that they are ignorant and that they have an evil nature. Many social systems and institutions are based on these false beliefs. Excessive elitism, which is another element of expertise, is legitimised by the argument that the majority of people are incapable of managing their society and that they therefore need elites to rule them. Hence, the belief in ignorance, inability and the evil character of human nature have been used to legitimise social institutions on the basis of power. It is believed that humans are submissive to nature and that power is dominant. We can see this in the relationship between the state and the people, the party and party members, managers and workers, men and women within the family, and teachers and students.

Even when relationships should be based on friendship and love, beliefs of inability and deficiency still become legitimised to form a power relationship. For example, I have already mentioned that couples (men and women) are often not seen as a *tawheed* of excellence and talents. Here one should add that according to current social beliefs, a man and a woman are two imperfect beings that become perfect with marriage. What has been disregarded is the fact that two imperfect people could not become a perfect entity. Alternatively, women are viewed as incapable beings who become able through marriage and family. Even here, women are seen as seductive sexual objects who can be saved from seducing or being seduced by being within the family. It is obvious that the indicators of ability or disability are manifestations of power (e.g. money, position, authority of man over woman), despite the fact that human rights include both women's and men's rights.

Therefore, a discourse of freedom is of utmost importance because it is a discourse in which men and women can regain their dignity and intrinsic rights, abilities and talents. In this discourse it is not belief in evil nature or intrinsic inequality which forms the structure of the relationship. Those in the minority that sees itself as the basis of power will realise that they have deprived themselves of their human dignity. Those who play the role of the flock will realise that their role was based on neglect of their dignity, and that they have to take much more responsibility. To become conscious of the fact that we are entities who have rights and dignity and to believe that no one is born evil or a sinner, to become conscious of one's ability, talents and senses and hence to reconstruct social institutions based on this consciousness, is to develop along the right path, to recognise humanity in its totality.

12. Dignity will increase when identity is created in a nation, in the determination to live so that present moments embrace both past and future. Such a reconstruction of identity at both the individual and communal levels, in freedom, will increase dignity. Cultures will differ because they are the result of societies' attempts to develop in their specific homelands. In other words, culture is a creation and invention of people in a homeland. In order to understand this more fully, we must be able to separate culture from anti-culture and realise that anything which is produced by power should be perceived as anti-culture. By making this distinction, we will realise that we not only have 'a culture', but many different cultures (multi-cultures). We will also realise that there is a wide common denominator among cultures which they can share in a universal culture.

However, it is deceptive, a fantasy, to assume that one culture can become universal, as it would be an anti-culture which tries to present itself as culture and deceive the dominated. It would be a deception because culture is creation, and when one exchanges culture like borrowed clothes, it is no more than assimilation and a reduction of culture to assimilation. This approach will not create people with superior culture, but will instead create impotent people. If we just differentiate, as I have argued, between the products of culture and anti-culture, we will see that not much is left of cultures that are supposed to produce people with abilities, dignity and rights. We can see how societies are rapidly desertifying, and observe a massive increase in identity crises. The overall crisis will be unlike any other in human history. Hence, the task we should undertake in order to develop human dignity is to differentiate culture and anti-culture, and gradually limit the domain of power and increase the space for dignified human thought and activities in order to create an identity through development.

13. According to the Koran, human beings have accepted a trusteeship in freedom. In life, no responsibility is higher than leadership in freedom, and no trusteeship is superior to that of dignifying life via development in freedom. A human who neglects his/her spiritual side is also neglectful of his/her freedom and dignity. It also bears repeating that discourses of power have turned human beings as leaders into instruments of power and depleted the world of dignity. That is why, in order to recognise the dignity of other beings, a person with dignity needs a discourse of freedom as guiding principle.

14. Hence, if right aims to become the intermediary of humans, nature and the future, and humans aim to identify their right to dignity and nature, the contradiction which is currently the guiding principle of ideas and actions must be replaced with *tawheed*. Philosophies that perceive the material being as a product of contradiction have inevitably perceived humans as being determined

by mutual contradictions. Of course, they therefore cannot recognise freedom, rights and dignity. The truth is that to accept the principle of dichotomy and contradiction when these become guiding principles is a negation of human rights and dignity. That is why in the relationship between freedom and the guiding principles of dichotomy, this contradiction has been resolved by defining freedom based on power.

When the Prophet of Islam began his mission, the principle of dichotomy was not yet universal; in our time it has become so. Everywhere—between groups and between human societies and nature—we are at war with each other, and this war has brought the world to the brink of collapse. According to a Club of Rome report, humans and nature could be in the last stages of their life (Von Weizsäcker 2009). That prediction is reminiscent of the Koran's description of groups and cities which were destroyed when they did not turn from dichotomous principles to *tawheed*.

> Such were the 'Ad people: They rejected the Signs of their Lord and Cherisher; disobeyed His Apostles; And followed the command of every powerful, obstinate transgressor. ... To the Thamud People (We sent) Salih, one of their own brethren. He said: 'O my people! Worship God! Ye have no other god but Him. It is He Who hath produced you from the earth and settled you therein; then ask forgiveness of Him, and turn to Him (in repentance): for my Lord is (always) near, ready to answer. ... Oh my people! This she-camel of God is a symbol to you: leave her to feed on God's (free) earth, and inflict no harm on her, or a swift penalty will seize you!' But they did ham-string her. So [Salih] said: 'Enjoy yourselves in your homes for three days: (Then will be your ruin): (Behold) there a promise not to be belied!' When Our Decree issued We saved Salih and those who believed with him by (special) Grace from Ourselves − and from the Ignominy of that day. For thy Lord − He is the Strong One, and able to enforce His Will. The (mighty) Blast overtook the wrong-doers, and they lay prostrate in their homes before the morning. (Koran 11:59, 61, 64−67)

After the Hud people, the people of Ad and Thamud also replaced *tawheed* with unipolar dichotomy.[11] They neglected their dignity and sought pleasure in dominating others and destroying animals and nature. Even when the last day came, they closed their eyes and ears to warnings until death overtook their towns.

When we compare the principle which we can extract from these verses with the Club of Rome report cited above, one fundamental difference becomes apparent: the report's authors neglected the fact that in today's world, the guiding principle of individuals, groups and nations has become dichotomy. Therefore, their warning will get nowhere if people fail to realise that the source of their destructive attitudes is the dichotomous nature of the principles guiding their thinking and action.

In 1463, Giovanni Pico della Mirandola based his work *On the Dignity of Man* on a saying: 'there is nothing to be seen more wonderful than man' (Pico della Mirandola 2012: 109). He argued that this was the best description of humanism (see also Godin & Margolin nd). However, he neglected the fact that humans seek dignity through *tawheed*, freedom and rights. A large number of cultures and all parts of the culture which we call the culture of life are based on the principle of *tawheed*. The products of power are anti-culture, and they erode human beings

---

[11]'Unipolar dichotomy' refers to a dichotomous relationship in which one pole is dominant.

because they lead them to neglect their dignity, rights, talents and abilities and reduce them to robots. This is happening to such an extent that today, a majority of people are unable to see the death of nature and fail to remember a basic fact of humanity that was immortalised in a poem by Sadi, a 13th-century Iranian poet. Sadi wrote that 'all men are members of the same body, created from one essence. If fate brings suffering to one member, the other cannot stay at rest. You who remain indifferent to the burden of the pain of others do not deserve to be called human' (Arberry 1945).

Before it is too late, before the principle of dichotomy, which functions as a despotic, stubborn, obstinate principle, comes to dominate all life, return to *tawheed* and find your true dignity.

The destruction from lack of *tawheed* and true dignity touched my life personally (*writes Abol-Hassan Bani-Sadr, co-author of this book*). When Iraq attacked Iran in 1980, and I had to defend the country with an army that was nearly dismantled, I hoped to be killed many times rather than see the country overrun by the Iraqi army. I wished I had been killed when my helicopter crashed, and not seen those days. However, because of my belief in life and dignity, I came to my senses and was filled with belief. I reproached myself for my death wish and found a solution by reminding myself of the dignity, courage, and ability of Iranian soldiers and officers. Astonishingly, despite the general belief that Iran would be defeated, not only was Iran not overrun by the Iraqi army, but the destiny of the war was changed in its first months. Therefore, I am well aware that it is hard to resist power in the search for dignity. However, by resisting these passing sentiments, one can transform them into eternity.

References

Admin (2007) The list: the world's fastest-growing religions. Foreign Policy, 13 May. http://www.foreignpolicy.com/articles/2007/05/13/the_list_the_worlds_fastest_growing_religions

Arberry A (1945) Kings and beggars: the first two chapters of Sadi's Gulestan. Luzac and Co., London

Armstrong K (2001) Islam: a short history. Phoenix Press, London

Bani-Sadr A (1992) Osoole Raahnemaye Eslam (The guiding principles of Islam). Enghelab Eslami Publications

Esposito J (2011) What everyone needs to know about Islam. Oxford University Press, Oxford

Gaede P-M (2012) Editorial. So glaubt der Mensch, Geo Thema 3/12. Gruner & Jahr, Hamburg

Godin A, Margolin J-C (nd) Humanisme. In: Encyclopaedia Universalis. http://www.universalis.fr/encyclopedie/humanisme/

Halm H (2011) Der Islam: Geschichte und Gegenwart. Beck, Munich

Hershock P (2003) Buddhist philosophy as a Buddhist practice. In: Solomon R and Higgins K (eds) From Africa to Zen. Rowman and Littlefield, Lanham, p 239–254

Lanczkowski G (1989) Geschichte der nichtchristlichen Religionen. Fischer, Frankfurt

Pico della Mirandola G (2012) Oration on the dignity of man (Oratio de hominis dignitate). Edited by F Borghesi, M Papio, M Riva. Cambridge University Press, New York

Reuter C (2012) Die Macht des Propheten. In: So glaubt der Mensch, Geo Thema 3/12. Gruner & Jahr, Hamburg, p 76–95

Shariati A (1979) On the sociology of Islam: lectures by Ali Shariati. Mizan Press, New York
Sinai N (2012) Die heilige Schrift des Islams. Herder, Freiburg
Von Weizsäcker E (2009) Introduction. In: Von Weizsäcker E, Hargroves K, Smith MH, Desha C,
    Stasinopoulos P. Factor five: transforming the global economy through 80% improvements in
    resource productivity. Earthscan, London, p 1–19 http://www.naturaledgeproject.net/
    Documents/F500Introduction.pdf
Weitz B (2011) Nachgefragt: Weltreligionen. Zentralen fuer Politische Bildung, Berlin.

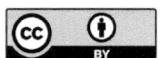

Chapter 4
Middle East and West: Can Common Ground Be Found?

Abstract This chapter argues that one can find an inner kernel in dignity discussions that unites major Western and Middle Eastern streams: dignity as a sense of self-worth, which we have a duty to develop and respect in ourselves and a duty to protect in others. At the same time, it is stressed that this book identified a range of diverse interpretations of dignity. For meaningful dialogue on the subject, it is therefore necessary to listen carefully and ascertain whether conversation partners are using the same or at least a similar concept of dignity. If not, fundamental disagreements can remain hidden to the detriment of constructive consensus.

Keywords Dignity · Middle east · Dialogue · Self-worth

The Western concept of dignity has six very different interpretations, if one includes dignity as slogan.

- Dignity as virtue: showing resilience, acceptance, poise, patience and endurance in the face of hardship, for instance.
- Dignity as rank and position: the dignity of a senior politician or a senior cleric, for instance.
- Dignity as comportment: not shouting and smoking in maternity wards, for instance.
- Dignity as understood by Kant and expressed through his formula of humanity: those who have dignity can expect (or command as Kant would say) respect for their reasonable sense of purpose and self-worth.
- God-given dignity: dignity equated with a sanctity of life as, for instance, in Catholicism.
- Dignity as slogan: this cannot be defined precisely, but can be found in highly charged debates, for instance against new technologies,[1] which are seen as an affront against human dignity.

---

[1]Kettner (2004) provides a good example, using dignity discussions in the context of embryonic stem cell research.

© The Author(s) 2017
D. Schroeder and A. Bani-Sadr, *Dignity in the 21st Century*,
SpringerBriefs in Philosophy, DOI 10.1007/978-3-319-58020-3_4

The two main philosophical streams of Western dignity are dignity as virtue and dignity realised through the formula of humanity. We have extracted from them a common core, namely a sense of self-worth. Could this extension be applied to the Middle Eastern concept? Yes. Dignity as respect for and the protection of the self-worth of human beings is the core that could harmonise the main Western approaches to dignity with the Koranic interpretation.

The Koran, as interpreted in this book, encourages its readers to replace humiliation with dignity, leading to a deviolentisation of life. Dignity leads to peace, according to the Koran. In humiliating others, the Koran argues, one loses one's own dignity. It also asks followers to develop their own dignity first, as a basis for recognising the dignity of others and acting upon this recognition. No one can revoke one's own dignity, the Koran argues, but oneself. Recognising and developing one's abilities, talents and senses belongs to the search for dignity. At the same time, one can help others develop and assist in their self-improvement and quest for dignity. Finally, striving towards dignity, according to the Koran, means that people need to be aware of their spiritual dimension and develop their related abilities in a constant effort to improve themselves. For instance, the inferiority of the social standing of women is an indication of social decadence and a sign that men's dignity is not developed.

From the above, one can see a strong similarity between dignity in the Koran and dignity as virtue, and in particular a strong emphasis on developing self-worth and assisting others in doing so. Human dignity is contingent upon the recognition of one's own nobility (self-worth) and others' nobility. Neglect of other people's dignity is a result of the neglect of one's own, according to the Koran. For instance, corruption is an example of neglect for one's own dignity.

At the outset of the book we quoted Fukuyama's (2012) editorial commenting on the Arab Spring. He wrote: 'The basic issue was one of *dignity*, or the lack thereof, the feeling of worth or self-esteem that all of us seek.'

It thus seems that one can find an inner kernel in dignity discussions that unites major Western and Middle Eastern streams: dignity as a sense of self-worth, which we have a duty to develop and respect in ourselves and a duty to protect in others.

At the same time, this book identified a range of diverse interpretations of dignity. For meaningful dialogue on the subject, it is therefore necessary to listen carefully and ascertain whether conversation partners are using the same or at least a similar concept of dignity. If not, fundamental disagreements can remain hidden to the detriment of constructive consensus.

We would like to end with a fictional dialogue.

4.1   Dignity—A Fictional Dialogue

Doris Schroeder talking to a friend, a psychiatrist.

Friend: Did you ever write that book on dignity you told me about?

Doris: *Yes.*
With Bani-Sadr?
Yes.
How was it?
I am glad I didn't write the book on my own.
Why?
I now have a stronger belief in the value of being precise, commonsensical and analytical in applied ethics and a stronger view on the limitations of this approach.
Why?
People often seem to make moral decisions based on unquestioned assumptions. And they mostly see their own situation and outlook. If one combines this attitude with a lack of empathy for others, some serious misjudgements can result.
Do you have an example?
There was one case I used for the book that I found profoundly sad and worrying. It was discussed using the term 'dignity'. A 28-year old woman went to court to have her feeding tubes removed because she wanted to die.
Why?
She was suffering from a painful illness and was also quadriplegic.
What did the court decide?
They granted her request and allowed the removal of the tubes. She died.
Did you think this was wrong?
No. On the contrary, I do believe it is wrong to force artificial nutrition on somebody against their will.
So what was wrong?
The way the court approached the decision. And the obvious hidden assumptions the judges must have had.
What do you mean?
The judges showed no empathy with the young woman—who was called Elizabeth. They simply imagined what they *would feel like if they were to go from presiding over a court to being quadriplegic and in pain.*
And?
Their written judgement said that Elizabeth was 'imprisoned and must lie physically helpless subject to the ignominy, embarrassment, humiliation and dehumanizing aspects created by her helplessness'.
I see what you mean.
To focus almost exclusively on Elizabeth's helplessness and toileting needs under the topic of dignity is just wrong.
And what does this have to do with your belief in the value of analytical precision?
An applied ethicist who tries to be precise and starts from everyday occurrences or literature can bring out various dimensions in a concept, for instance in dignity.
Hmmm.
Dignity is often mentioned in the context of the dependency of severely ill or disabled people ...

And?

And, I wish there was another word in this context. It seems wrong—to me—to use the word dignity both for Nelson's Mandela's comportment on Robben Island and in the context of incontinence.

I see.

It becomes dangerous when a concept that is imbued with almost mystical powers, such as the constitutional right to the inviolability of dignity, is suddenly used by judges who are pronouncing their views on the alleged humiliation of incontinence.

Don't you understand the judges?

Yes, I do. But I believe that this is not right.

Let me read you something. It is about an old man talking to a middle-aged man over a chess game. The old man had been involved in the resistance against Salazar in Portugal. [She produces a paperback and then reads the excerpt given in this book's introduction about the old man in a nursing home and his Swiss visitor (Mercier 2009: 364–365)].

You aren't saying anything… It is moving, isn't it?

Yes.

This man who had risen above his torturers despite unbearable agony could not cope with incontinence. The other man, Gregorius, analyses what dignity means for him and concludes: 'And then you get worked up about a dirtied bed?'

Who is the author?

He is Peter Bieri, a Swiss professor of moral philosophy, but he writes novels under the pseudonym Pascale Mercier. What counts, though, is not the author but his main character. What Gregorius does show, in my view, is the value of precision and analysing concepts in applied ethics.

Yes?

Gregorius showed Eça that his intuitions about dignity and comportment and incontinence were incompatible with other understandings of dignity that he himself had adopted in an extreme situation.

And is that what your book is about? Showing the difference between these two concepts of dignity? The one about incontinence … well, you know what I mean, and the one about resisting torture?

Yes, that's part of what I tried to do in my sections of the book. I termed one 'comportment dignity' and the other 'dignity as virtue', but …

Wait a second… [She opens the paperback again.] *Let me read something else to you. This time Gregorius is listening to a medical doctor:*

> The day before, I had informed a patient in the presence of his wife that he didn't have long to live. You have to, I had persuaded myself before I called the two of them into the consulting room, they have to plan for themselves and the five children—and anyway: part of human dignity consists of the strength to look your fate, even a hard one, in the eye. … I took off my glasses and pinched the bridge of my nose between thumb and forefinger before I spoke. The two must have recognized the gesture as a harbinger of an awful truth, for when I looked up, they had grasped each other's hands, which looked as if they hadn't sought each other for decades. (Mercier 2009: 79–80)

Yes?

That's a form of dignity as virtue, dignity in the face of hardship.

So are these the variations of dignity you came up with?

No, there are five, plus one outlier.

Five??!!

Yes. But don't let me bore you with the details. What I hope to have shown is that these five concepts are strong and meaningful for many people and that they can contradict each other. It is therefore important to define them properly and make sure that discussants are talking about the same thing. And then there is a sixth one, dignity as slogan, which is indeed not meaningful.

How do you mean, 'discussants'?

I mean people who are arguing about specific moral dilemmas, for instance, end-of-life decisions. If one is talking about comportment dignity and the other about a concept inspired by Catholic belief, which implies the sanctity of life, they will talk past each other.

Talk past each other?

One more. [Doris opens the paperback again.] *Here is Gregorius once more.*

> I sat down in the lecture hall next to the Irish man. ... It was unbelievable. The lecturer. ... sketched in a creaky voice a casuistic of lying that couldn't have been more nitpicking or farther from reality. ... Can God create a stone He couldn't lift? If not, then He isn't almighty, if yes, then He isn't either, for now there is a stone He cannot lift. That was the kind of scholasticism that poured forth into the room. ... But that wasn't what was really unbelievable. What was really incomprehensible was the discussion, as it was called. Cast into and enclosed in the gray lead frame of polite empty ... phrases, the people spoke perfectly past one another. Constantly they said they understood each other, answered each other. But it wasn't so. Not one, not a single one of the discussants, showed the slightest indication of a change of mind in view of the reasons presented. (Mercier 2009: 136–137)

If it goes well, analysing in applied ethics can illuminate concepts and help people avoid talking past each other. If that happens, people will change their minds, at least some of them. There will be some movement.

Does that work?

Not if people's attitudes and opinions are narcistically cemented in stone and they are unwilling to listen to others.

So?

In addition to the analysis, there has to be a willingness to open one's mind to others.

Is that where the limitations are?

Pardon?

You talked about the limitations of analytical philosophy before.

Yes.

That's interesting.

I don't know how one can instil a sense of empathy and imaginative caring in human beings, for instance in the judges who presided over Elizabeth's fate. But I know that a sole focus on rational analysis will not suffice for fully rounded, well-balanced human interactions. But then, you *are the psychiatrist.*

And how does this relate to the book?

Do you remember something else I said earlier on?

What?

That I would like to co-author with an eminent scholar from an ancient culture, a highly respected politician known around the world?

Yes?

An excellent counterbalance against over-rationalising is input from a source that provides reflective scholarship rooted in a different culture, don't you think?

Hmmm.

I have been lucky that Abol-Hassan Bani-Sadr co-authored this book.

Why?

Don't you think so?

I just want to understand better what you mean.

But I already told you that wisdom and scholarship balance against over-rationalising. They make you think. Especially if you don't understand everything immediately.

Hmmm. Perhaps you need to tell me more about the limitations of the analytical approach.

I believe there are three. The first is that one still needs judgement.

How do you mean?

Analytical philosophy cannot easily justify a preference between two equally coherent thought systems—for instance, to decide between dignity as virtue and dignity according to Kant if they were applied in specific cases.

Yes, I see what you mean. And the second limitation?

Perhaps that's not really a limitation of analytical philosophy, more a limitation of analytical people who fail to show any empathy or common sense.

Empathy? Common sense? Are you thinking about changing careers and moving into my domain?

[Doris smiles.] *Let me read something to you, written by a colleague of yours but for an applied ethics journal.*

> One case of mental disorder was encountered by a friend of mine, in an interview with a woman who had killed her infant. When asked why she had done it she gave the following explanation.
>
> 1. All human beings die and are judged
> 2. They are judged according to their sins
> 3. If they are found innocent, they live with God in heaven
> 4. Living with God in heaven is better than life on earth
> 5. My baby has committed no sins
> 6. If he dies, he will be innocent and go to heaven
> 7. Therefore, I killed my baby.
>
> While it is clear that there is irrationality of a very profound kind here, it is not clear just how to categorise it. Premises 1, 2, and 3 are believed by a great many people and therefore each belief is 'one ordinarily accepted by other members of the person's culture or sub-culture.' Premise 4 is found in some of the great religious works of Western Culture (e.g. Paul, Philippians 1:21). Premise 5 is a plausible premise on most readings by people who think in those terms, and 6 is merely a logical entailment of 2, 3, and 5. The practical

conclusion comes as a surprise but, given the argument, the surprise is not explicable on purely rational grounds because the conclusion follows from premises that are widely believed by rational people. Nevertheless, we are not surprised that the argument was produced in justification by a woman accused of child murder and thought, by a psychiatrist examining her, to be suffering from psychosis. (Gillett 2003)

Do you see what I mean?

Yes.

I believe an over-emphasis on rationality and logic alone is detrimental in applied ethics, even if the degree is obviously different from the above disorder. But, for instance, it is not clear to me why philosophers do not work more often with psychologists and psychiatrists. On the topic of dignity that might be very fruitful.

Why?

Bani-Sadr and I came to the conclusion that there is an inner kernel that binds together the two main Western conceptions of dignity (dignity as virtue and the Kantian understanding of not instrumentalising other people) and dignity as seen in the Koran. It is dignity as a sense of self-worth, which we have a duty to develop and respect in ourselves and a duty to protect in others.

How could psychologists or psychiatrists help?

You know that, don't you?

I do, but I am interested to hear what you think.

I found an interesting analysis of human dignity in a psychology book. What the psychologists did was to name the four scourges that harm dignity (Fig. 4.1). The first scourge is violence. Those humans who can defend themselves against violence can protect their dignity, but if you are a child, for instance, or a person who

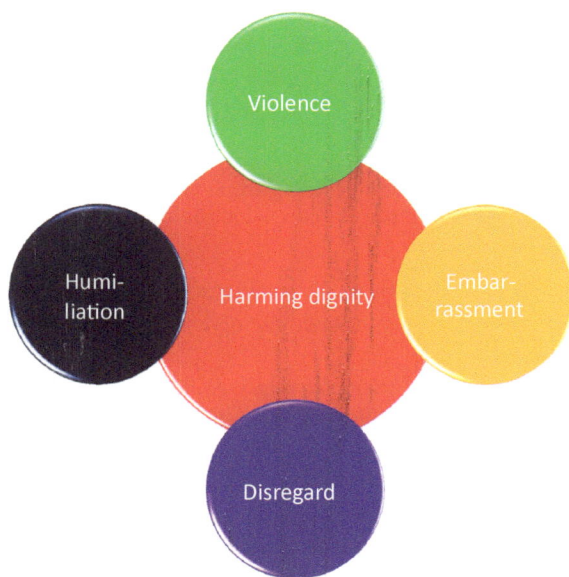

Fig. 4.1 Harming dignity: the four scourges

cannot escape for some reason, constant violence will make you feel smaller and smaller and ever more helpless, until, in the end, you have lost your sense of self-worth. Let me read something from the book:

> Somebody who is regularly unable to defend themselves tends towards losing all hope of a solution or exit and starts to accept the loss of self-worth and the sense of dignity. How are you meant to feel when you are beaten all the time and when your personal boundaries are not respected? Losing your sense of self-worth can become natural, and helplessness becomes the terrible normality. (Baer and Frick-Baer 2009: 12, DS translation)

The second scourge is humiliation. That is something philosophers have worked on in relation to dignity, especially an Israeli philosopher called Margalit. But it was still good to see it in the psychology book. The authors say that humiliation begins where people are made smaller through words or behaviour. They give the example of a boy who hears all the time: 'You'll be nobody, you'll end up as a bin man,' and loses all sense of self-worth over the years (Baer and Frick-Baer 2009: *13). They write*:

> Humiliations are part of everyday life for many people. If they happen only occasionally, people can normally defend themselves successfully and can find a way to cope with the denigration. The main danger occurs in the repetition and in the continuity. Where people are continuously subjected to humiliation, this experience trickles into their image of themselves and the sense of one's own dignity can get lost. (Baer and Frick-Baer 2009: 15, DS translation)

The third scourge is disregard. Do you agree with this one? It doesn't seem as obvious to me as the others:

> From a psychological perspective, it is obvious. Humans are very social beings; to be ignored and disregarded systematically is very difficult for the human psyche. (Baer and Frick-Baer 2009: 15, DS translation)

That's what the psychologists in the book say. They give a case example where parents ignored their child for a week after some wrongdoing or after a low grade at school. And the child said 'I was treated like thin air for a week. That was terrible. I yearned to be shouted at.' (Baer and Frick-Baer 2009: *16, DS translation). The psychologists write*:

> To be ignored and not to receive answers or comments to what one says – these are heavy punishments and they can make people suffer a lot. (Baer and Frick-Baer 2009: 16, DS translation)

The fourth scourge is embarrassment. To me that sounded a lot like the second one, humiliation, but the examples given made the difference clear. What do you think? What were the examples?
One case recalled how a child was constantly embarrassed and on edge because the father regularly got drunk in public. She said, 'When my father had one of his binges, I was so incredibly ashamed. I found this so undignified. ... Later I despised him. And I had terrible stomach pains. ... A little bit of my dignity died in my stomach.' (Baer and Frick-Baer 2009: *18, DS translation)*
Yes, that's a good example. Humiliation is usually meant when a particular person is targeted, but you can feel serious embarrassment unrelated to yourself, or at least not directly related to yourself, as in this case (Fig. 4.1).

The other reason I liked the analysis from the psychologists was the obvious link to Bani-Sadr's thoughts on dignity. They spoke about power, as he did. There is one section in particular, where Bani-Sadr writes that freedom and human rights will become casualties if human relationships are built on power.

And the psychologists?

They write that many people who feel defenceless and vulnerable do so because other people's power has wounded them permanently through humiliation and violations of dignity.

So, yes, I can see how this is all coming together: dignity according to the Koran, dignity as virtue, dignity as not instrumentalising others. So what next?

This is probably the place where one should ask, 'Which book next?'

And?

I think my answer to 'What next?' is 'Do something practical, don't just write about it.'

References

Baer U, Frick-Baer G (2009) Würde und Eigensinn. Beltz Verlag, Weinheim: p. 12. DS translation
Fukuyama F (2012) The drive for dignity. Foreign Policy, 12 January. http://foreignpolicy.com/2012/01/12/the-drive-for-dignity/
Gillett G (2003) Reasoning in bioethics. Bioethics 17(3):243–260
Kettner M (ed) (2004) Biomedizin und Menschenwürde. Suhrkamp, Frankfurt
Mercier P (2009) Night train to Lisbon. Atlantic Books, London

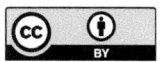

Index

© The Author(s) 2017
D. Schroeder and A. Bani-Sadr, *Dignity in the 21st Century*,
SpringerBriefs in Philosophy, DOI 10.1007/978-3-319-58020-3

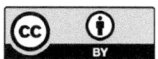